MEATLESS
IN
COWTOWN

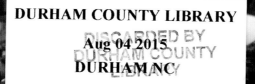

MEATLESS IN COWTOWN

A Vegetarian Guide to Food and Wine, Texas-Style

Laura Samuel Meyn
and Anthony Head

PHOTOGRAPHY BY
Jason Varney

RUNNING PRESS
PHILADELPHIA · LONDON

Published by Running Press,
A Member of the Perseus Books Group

Printed in China

Books published by Running Press are available at special discounts for bulk purchases in the United States by corporations, institutions, and other organizations. For more information, please contact the Special Markets Department at the Perseus Books Group, 2300 Chestnut Street, Suite 200, Philadelphia, PA 19103, or call (800) 810-4145, ext. 5000, or e-mail special.markets@perseusbooks.com.

ISBN 978-0-7624-5308-5

Library of Congress Control Number: 2014956653

E-book ISBN 978-0-7624-5601-7

9 8 7 6 5 4 3 2 1
Digit on the right indicates the number of this printing

Design by Joshua McDonnell
Edited by Sophia Muthuraj
Typography: Avenir and Lato
Food and Prop Stylist: Carrie Ann Purcell
Cover illustration by Christian Cantiello of Keystone Sign & Company

Running Press Book Publishers
2300 Chestnut Street
Philadelphia, PA 19103-4371

Visit us on the web!
www.offthemenublog.com

To Till, Samuel, and Susanna—where would this book be without your healthy appetites, your honest feedback, and your declarations of "In the book!" when a recipe was especially successful? Thank you for being both critics and fans, and for bringing to our table such overwhelming enthusiasm for Texas-inspired meatless meals.

—Laura

This work is dedicated with love and affection to Michele, the true epicurean of the family.

—Anthony

CONTENTS

ACKNOWLEDGMENTS

Together, we're grateful to editors Sophia Muthuraj and Kristen Green Wiewora at Running Press, who took a risk on a quirky idea when others doubted the value of a vegetarian cookbook from Texas—and to our agent, friend, and fellow Texan Martha Hopkins, who believed from the beginning. We'd also like to toast designer Joshua McDonnell, photographer Jason Varney, stylist Carrie Ann Purcell, and sign painter Christian Cantiello for embracing the project and making it so beautiful. And finally, our heartfelt thanks to the sanity-saving recipe testers—Katherine Brown, Michele Head, Till Meyn, Virginia Meyn, Hanna Page, and Susan Samuel—who came to the rescue when we needed extra hands.

INTRODUCTION

Meatless in Cowtown is a personal collection of Texas-inspired recipes from two vegetarian friends and food writers who moved to the Lone Star State. Although Texas is not generally considered to be vegetarian-friendly, its ingredients and techniques offer a surprising capacity for meatless meals; we've even included several vegan and gluten-free recipes. This book was born out of many years of cooking, eating, and drinking together; our mission is to share vegetarian meals that are delicious, celebratory, and unexpectedly Texan.

We've both been in Texas for close to a decade, but we've been meatless even longer. Laura was sixteen when—looking at her mother over a half-eaten chicken pot pie—she came out as a vegetarian. The signs were all there—the early love of E. B. White's *Charlotte's Web*; the uncommonly strong bond with the family dog; the shrimping adventures at the ancestral family house by the bay in Alabama, where it was her self-appointed job to throw back into the water the gasping fish that had been caught in the nets. Laura's mother bought her a copy of *Recipes for a Small Planet*, and, over the next couple years with her sister away at college and her father stationed overseas, they often went meatless together. (Her mother was pleased to discover that it

measurably lowered her cholesterol.) Soon Laura was poring over cookbooks by Mollie Katzen and Anna Thomas. She fell for Till, the man she would marry, when he made her a vegetable quiche; she even forgave him for baking the next one in a graham cracker crust.

Anthony was born and raised in southern Indiana and graduated from Indiana University, in Bloomington. But he owes his real education to time spent tending bar at the Blue Bird, where he developed quick judgment, independent thinking, and creativity. He took those skills to Chicago and continued as a barkeep at a pizza restaurant on the north side. When he arrived in Los Angeles a couple of years later, he found that all the bartending jobs were taken by actors, so he turned to his other ambition, writing, and landed a job with *Bon Appétit* magazine in 1994.

While researching a story on the link between red meat and cancer, he learned that one of his favorite musicians, Frank Zappa, had died of prostate cancer. That day Anthony gave up eating red meat. When his dad was diagnosed with prostate cancer in 1995, he gave up chicken and other fowl. And when he became a dog owner, well, he gave up eating anything that could choose to save its own life—meat, poultry, and seafood. His first dog has since moved on to the great dog park in the sky; happily, his father is still around and cancer-free.

Our friendship began shortly after we met in 1997 as the only vegetarians on *Bon Appétit*'s editorial team. We learned much about entertaining and the culinary arts during one of the country's more explosive and innovative periods (think Alice Waters, Wolfgang Puck, Charlie Trotter). Laura took a professional pastry course, and hung around the *Bon Appétit* test kitchen, asking questions about techniques and ingredients. Perhaps it was foreshadowing events to come, but before leaving the magazine, she shifted her focus into the cookbook division. Anthony focused on health and nutrition writing and began editing the wine, spirits, and beer stories as well.

While meatless dining was growing as a trend at the millennium's close, it was far from mainstream; *Bon Appétit* certainly wasn't devoting too many stories to vegetarianism. Although we were respected for our writing, editing, and even recipe contributions, we both remained somewhat marginalized professionally for our dietary decisions. (We were frequently "excused" from the meatier tastings in the test kitchen.)

Within a few years, Anthony married Laura's closest friend at *Bon Appétit*, Michele, who worked in the art department. Till, Laura's husband, briefly joined the ranks of Condé Nast (*Bon Appétit*'s parent company), spending the summer between graduate school and professorial life doing fact-checking for *Architectural Digest*, which was just one floor up. The four of us hiked in the Hollywood Hills after work, bringing along baguettes stuffed with pesto, fresh mozzarella, and tomatoes, and, always, a couple bottles of wine. We also vacationed together on the Central Coast, cooking up big breakfasts that fueled long beach walks.

Today, we both still write professionally about the good things in life—and we're thriving as vegetarians in Texas, although we initially thought it would be a bit challenging. For one thing, Laura's adopted hometown, Fort Worth, calls itself "Cowtown," a shout-out to the cattle industry that helped build the city and the state. To this day, Fort Worth still drives cattle through the streets (to be clear, it's for the tourists), and it still boasts quite a reputation for being a place to find a damn good steak. But in spite of concerns from good-hearted pals around the country, she's just fine—and finely fed—in Texas.

So is Anthony, who lives with his wife, Michele, just outside of the San Marcos city limits in Hays County between Austin and San Antonio. In this southern edge of the Hill Country, the air is always heavy with the lingering aromas from the many local barbecue pits (as well as the constant sound of gunshots during deer season).

And now, in Texas, whenever our families get together for a summer float down the San Marcos River (we Texans gleefully call this "toobing") or a weekend in Fort Worth, what we're going to eat and drink always plays a big part in the fun. We've experimented with making homemade corn tortillas, debated the easiest way to roast chiles, and discussed the

old-fashioned charm of buttermilk pie. And we pour wines and beers and spirits—more and more of them from Texas.

Professionally, we have met plenty of chefs, winemakers, bread bakers, brewers, farmers, and distillers, as well as countless Texans who aren't eating meat three meals a day. The state boasts several of the nation's largest and fastest-growing cities, attracting myriad culinary influences from afar, many of which use meat sparingly. At the same time, we've seen how the farm-to-table dining philosophies have spread from small towns to the big cities and back again, expanding the use and availability of fresh, local ingredients everywhere.

While Fort Worth's nickname so succinctly sums up our state's meat-loving reputation, it's not the only cow in the corral. Columbus, Ohio, and Wichita, Kansas, also call themselves "Cowtown." In Northern California, halfway between Sacramento and San Francisco, is Vacaville (for the non-Spanish speaker, that's "Cowtown"). In fact, we've both come to see the whole United States—metaphorically, of course—as Cowtown.

And yet, we've found that our fellow Texans are a lot more forward-thinking, creative, and open-minded than they're usually given credit for—and that goes double at dinnertime. Around town and around the state, Texas chefs are happy to oblige us with meatless meals—although it always helps to have a sense of humor (and irony) intact—and, of course, to ask nicely. So we've even included a few chef and mixologist recipes from some of the people we've met along our journey.

Over the years, we've discovered that vegetarians like us are heartily welcomed at the dinner table in the great state of Texas, which is why we welcome everyone to ours.

LAURA ON FOOD

The recipes: This book offers a vegetarian take on Texas home-style cooking, which means big, bold flavors—and nothing fussy or formal. Our recipes make use of ingredients that are abundant in Texas, from pecans to peaches to sweet potatoes. Several of the recipes also give a nod to Texas's love affair with Mexican food. But the most important requirement we set for these recipes is that our friends and family—and most aren't vegetarian—love them as much as we do.

Defining diets: I'm not vegan, gluten-free, or kosher. But having been vegetarian for more than twenty years, I pay attention to other people's diets. Here's how we define various diets:

Vegetarian. All of the recipes in this book are vegetarian—meaning there is no meat, fowl, or fish in them. We do use dairy, eggs, and honey in some of the recipes.

Kosher. Those who keep kosher know their own standards best, but any vegetarian recipe that doesn't rely on nonkosher packaged ingredients can be prepared as kosher with the proper pans and utensils. That's pretty much every recipe in this book.

Vegan. Vegan recipes are purely plant-based, meaning everything in them is derived from grains, seeds, nuts, fruits, or vegetables. Strict vegans and those cooking for them will want to check all packaged ingredients carefully. For example, while many brands of semisweet and dark chocolate chips have dairy in them, several do not. The store brand at Whole Foods offers vegan chocolate chips, as do Enjoy Life and SunSpire. Scharffen Berger and the store brands at Costco and Trader Joe's have vegan chocolate chips, too, but sometimes with the disclaimer that while the product is dairy-free the processing happens on the same equipment as products that contain dairy (and other allergens). An alternative is to buy a vegan chocolate bar (many high-quality dark chocolates are naturally vegan) and coarsely chop it to use in place of the chocolate chips. In this book, vegan recipes are indicated with a **V**. Recipes that contain optional adaptions for vegans (choose your ingredients and garnishes accordingly) are marked **Vegan Option**.

Gluten-free. Gluten-free recipes avoid using a protein found in wheat, rye, and barley. What complicates the diet is the cross-contamination that often happens during food processing and even in-home food preparation, tainting otherwise gluten-free foods. For example, putting flour tortillas on the same cutting board as corn tortillas is enough to make some people sick for days. If you follow a gluten-free diet or are cooking for someone who does, it's important to carefully check any packaged ingredients to make sure that they are certified gluten-free—oatmeal, cornstarch, baking powder, and more—and to use care in your food preparation to avoid cross-contamination (for more, visit gfco.org or celiaccentral.org). In this book, recipes that are gluten-free are indicated with **GF**. Recipes that offer alternatives to make them gluten-free are marked **Gluten-Free Option**.

Produce shopping: Cooking seasonally—with produce that's at its most flavorful, most abundant, and least expensive—is probably the single surest way to keep your standards high and your budget low. Keeping it local matters, too. Beyond shopping the farmers' markets, which we highly recommend, one label that's helpful here in the Lone Star State is the "Go Texan" logo. Instituted by the Texas Department of Agriculture, this campaign promotes the "products, culture, and communities" of Texas, which we're proud to point out includes an awful lot of produce. The vast majority of our ingredients for testing these recipes came with a Go Texan logo, including tofu, zucchini, beer, chiles, tortillas, blood oranges, cheeses, pecans, tomatoes,

berries, wines, kale, corn, brown rice, and all sorts of herbs. Because Texas is such a huge producer of fruits and vegetables, there's always something just coming into season to try. We often turn to Go Texan's Texas Produce Availability Chart, which helps determine when a specific ingredient is in season. You can find it at GoTexan.org.

Organic baking: Throughout this book, the recipes call for organic granulated sugar. This ingredient is a light caramel color and has a slight caramel taste. Without getting into too many unsavory details, the granulated white sugar most of us grew up with isn't always considered to be vegetarian, because some companies process theirs with "natural carbon"—also known as bone char. (As if you needed another reason to buy organic.) The recipes in this book also specify unbleached all-purpose flour; if you've ever noticed the pasty whiteness of baked goods at lower-echelon bakeries or donut shops, you recognize that keeping the chemicals out of the flour is a no-brainer for health as well as aesthetics. And to make my homemade sweets a little heartier, I often mix in some *white* whole wheat flour, which is produced from hard white whole wheat and offers a lighter texture than does the red whole wheat we're all used to.

ANTHONY ON ALCOHOL

What grows together goes together. That's classic food-and-wine pairing logic based on complementary flavor profiles developing organically around a region's natural resources. That philosophy fits right in with Texas because we produce many ingredients for wines, beers, and distilled spirits (not to mention juices and other nonalcoholic beverages). My palate is shaped by more than twenty years of on-the-job training, and along the way I have come to discern and truly appreciate a sense of place through the craftsmanship of regional products. To complement many of the recipes here, I've included suggestions for Texas wine and beer pairings, which readers can use as a guideline for finding local libations wherever they live.

Texas wines: The most common question I get whenever I talk about Texas wines is: Texas makes wine? Yes. Texas and wine go way back—all the way back to the 1600s, when Spanish missionaries tended vineyards and made wine where El Paso stands today. Ever since then, family farmers lucky enough to find the right soil, fruit, and growing conditions have made Texas wine. Granted, many of those were on the sweet side and made from strawberries, cherries, peaches, and even wild mustang grapes.

Texas's modern winemaking era began in earnest in the mid-1960s, when the High Plains, Hill Country, and other parts of the state began experimenting commercially with grapes for producing fine, dry table wines. Today, Texas boasts more than 250 wineries, and Fredericksburg and the surrounding Hill Country is among the most popular domestic wine-tourism destinations outside of California's Napa Valley. So, yes. Texas does make wine.

The second thing I'm asked when I talk about Texas wines is: Are they any good? Yes. In fact, they're becoming respected outside the state and in other parts of the wine-loving world, due in part to an increase in knowledge by the grape growers and winemakers as well as planting the right grapes. Cabernet Sauvignon and Chardonnay grapes, which make the country's most popular red and white wines, don't express themselves in Texas the same way they do in California. However, Texas-grown Tempranillo, Viognier, Roussanne, Vermentino, and Tannat are crafted into wines with worldwide appeal. It's taking some time for Texans to learn and embrace these unfamiliar grapes, but they are being rewarded like never before in our state's long history of winemaking. So, yes. Texas wines are good. They're very good.

Texas craft beers: Texas is closing in on having one hundred small, independently owned craft breweries. While that number is impressive, it's also too low for my tastes. A state this size should have twice that many small breweries, which would mean more local beers to choose from when planning dinner.

However, I have no complaints whatsoever about the quality and appeal of Texas craft beers. We have talented, forward-thinking brewers who produce an extensive variety of finely crafted traditional beers while also pushing the envelope with exotic infusions—jalapeño ale or prickly pear lager, anyone?—and modernizing classic but forgotten styles, such as appealingly tart and food-friendly farmhouse ales.

Let me end with a quick word on temperature: When you're enjoying a fine Texas beer, do yourself a favor and skip the ice-cold mug. Or, at least, consider serving beer in only a *slightly* chilled mug. Beers can't open up into their full, fragrant potential when they're served too cold. Styles vary, of course, but most craft beers have ideal serving temperatures between 40 and 55 degrees Fahrenheit; generally speaking, the heavier the beer's body, the warmer the ideal serving temperature.

Texas spirits: Even though we are in the infancy of a new craft spirits boom (the first legal, post-Prohibition liquor distillery was set up in Texas in 1997), dozens of licensed distillers in Texas produce vodkas, rums, gins, whiskeys, and myriad liqueurs. As with the state's wine and beer industries, these companies are filled with people of passion and innovation, and many of them endeavor to use as many local and state ingredients in their products as possible. Whether you look for these spirited creations behind the bar, at your favorite club or restaurant, or in the liquor store to make drinks at home, they help put a delicious Texan spin to the occasion.

Alcohol for vegans: Everyone knows that wine is made from grapes, but far fewer understand that wine isn't necessarily vegan. Neither, for that matter, are beer and distilled spirits.

During both the beer-making and winemaking processes, "fining agents" are used to filter out tiny particles that cause beverages to appear cloudy. These fining agents include egg albumen, bone marrow, gelatin, and fish bladders. Although the finished wine or beer does not technically contain animal products, for vegans, the damage has already been done.

You won't be able to tell whether a beer or wine is vegan by its label—except in those cases when you can. A growing number of Texas winemakers and brewers who use non-animal-derived fining agents are clearly marking their bottles as "vegan."

The production of distilled spirits does not *generally* require such clarifying products, but dairy, honey, and other animal-derived ingredients may be used, though not always labeled. I do not distinguish between vegan and nonvegan alcohol products in this book.

SNACKS & STARTERS

GUACAMOLE WITH TOMATO
AND CILANTRO   20

FRESH TOMATO, CORN,
AND PEPPER SALSA   22

RESTAURANT-STYLE SMOKY RED SALSA   23

CLASSIC HUMMUS AND VARIATIONS   24

GARLICKY GARBANZO BEANS   26

SPICY PIMIENTO CHEESE WITH PECANS   27

ROASTED MIXED NUTS WITH ROSEMARY   28

CREAMY MUSHROOM PITA TRIANGLES   30

LEMONY DEVILED EGGS
WITH SPRING HERBS   31

NATURAL CHEDDAR AND JACK QUESO   33

NACHOS WITH REFRIED BEANS   34

REFRIED BEANS   35

GREENER GODDESS DIP
WITH FRESH VEGETABLES   36

BIG OL' ANTIPASTO PLATTER   39

GRILLED MULTIGRAIN CROSTINI   41

CHISHOLM TRAIL MIX   42

GRILLED EDAMAME   43

SAUTÉED OKRA WITH LEMON-CHIVE AÏOLI   44

LEMON-CHIVE AÏOLI   45

Salsa, guacamole, and queso to serve with tortilla chips; savory roasted nuts; fresh veggies and a deliciously herbed dip; and creamy mushrooms atop crispy pita. Sometimes a spread of vegetarian appetizers is less about being self-consciously vegetarian and more about serving a fabulous array of colors, tastes, and textures. Pair a few favorite snacks with a glass of Texas Viognier or something effervescent (whether sparkling wine or a crisp beer), and who needs meat—or dinner at all, really?

Guacamole with Tomato and Cilantro

Mashed avocados on their own, or maybe with a pinch of salt, are worth breaking out a bag of tortilla chips. But this guacamole with fresh lime juice, tomatoes, and cilantro takes it to the next level. When entertaining, make a generous amount—fresh guacamole tends to disappear quickly. In addition to being a delicious dip, guacamole also makes a great topping for veggie burgers, Mexican fare, and even omelets.

Makes about 4 cups guacamole :: **V • GF**

3 large Haas avocados (about 2 pounds)

½ cup minced sweet onion

½ cup seeded, finely chopped tomato

½ cup fresh cilantro leaves, chopped

2 tablespoons freshly squeezed lime juice

1 to 2 tablespoons minced seeded jalapeño pepper

¼ teaspoon kosher salt, or more to taste

Halve and pit the avocados; using a sharp knife, score a crosshatch pattern into the avocado flesh and squeeze it into a large bowl.

Add the onion, tomato, and cilantro. Pour the lime juice over the ingredients and stir with a fork, mashing the avocado coarsely and leaving some chunks.

Add 1 tablespoon of the jalapeño and ¼ teaspoon of salt; stir to combine.

Taste the guacamole and adjust the seasoning, adding additional jalapeño or salt, if desired. Serve at room temperature or chilled. Can be prepared up to 1 day ahead. Transfer the guacamole to a smaller bowl and cover with plastic wrap, pushing the plastic wrap down to touch the surface of the guacamole to prevent discoloration, and refrigerate for up to 1 day.

Fresh Tomato, Corn, and Pepper Salsa

Once you've made this colorful salsa cruda, store-bought salsa might not cut it anymore. Serve it simply with tortilla chips—or as a condiment with enchiladas, burritos, or quesadillas. Frozen corn kernels are a convenience item put to good use here; if it's corn season, use a couple of ears of fresh corn, either boiled for five minutes or briefly grilled before cutting the kernels from the cob. For extra protein, add 1½ cups of prepared black-eyed peas or black beans (or one 15-ounce can, drained and rinsed), and you'll have what some call "Cowboy Caviar," a recipe attributed to Helen Corbitt, the legendary former director of food for Dallas-based Neiman Marcus.

Makes 4 to 5 cups salsa : : **V • GF**

¼ cup freshly squeezed lime juice

¼ cup extra-virgin olive oil

2 teaspoons ground cumin

½ teaspoon kosher salt

1½ pounds tomatoes, seeded and finely chopped (about 3 cups)

1 cup frozen corn kernels, thawed

1 cup seeded finely chopped orange or red bell pepper (from about ½ large bell pepper)

¾ cup minced sweet onion (from about ½ medium-size onion)

2 medium-size jalapeño peppers, seeded and minced (about ¼ cup plus 2 tablespoons)

⅓ cup loosely packed fresh cilantro leaves, chopped

2 to 3 garlic cloves, finely minced

Whisk the lime juice, oil, cumin, and salt in a small bowl to blend.

Place the tomatoes, corn, bell pepper, onion, jalapeños, cilantro, and garlic in a large bowl; toss to combine.

Add the lime juice mixture and toss to coat. Serve the salsa at room temperature or chilled. Can be prepared up to 2 days ahead. Cover and refrigerate.

Restaurant-Style Smoky Red Salsa

Ridiculously quick and easy to make in a food processor or blender, this salsa will remind you of the simple but addictive variety that's served with chips before meals at your favorite Mexican restaurant. Salsa, of course, pairs well with any favorite corn chip—or as a condiment for breakfast, lunch, or dinner.

Makes about 2 cups salsa :: **V • GF**

1 (14.5-ounce) can fire-roasted diced tomatoes

½ cup coarsely chopped white onion

½ cup loosely packed fresh cilantro leaves

1 large jalapeño pepper, stemmed and coarsely sliced (leave seeds in)

1 whole chipotle chile in adobo sauce (from a 7-ounce can; gluten-free, if desired)

2 tablespoons freshly squeezed lime juice

1 to 2 small garlic cloves, peeled and smashed

½ teaspoon kosher salt, or more to taste

½ teaspoon ground cumin, or more to taste

Place all the ingredients in a blender or food processor. Blend until a chunky purée forms. Season to taste with additional salt and cumin, if desired. Cover and chill until cold, at least 1 hour. Serve cold. Can be prepared up to 3 days ahead. Keep refrigerated.

Classic Hummus and Variations

|||||||||||||||||||||||||||||||||||||||||||||||||||||||||||||||||||||||||||||||||||||||||||||||||||||||||||||||||||

Everyone needs a classic hummus recipe; the pure, simple rendition is my favorite. Using the from-scratch Garlicky Garbanzo Beans (page 26) not only gives you beans with better texture than you'd get from canned, it also leaves you with perfectly cooked garlic cloves to add to the mix; they offer plenty of flavor without the sharpness of their raw counterpart. The Roasted Red Pepper variation is smoky and sweet, and it's my children's favorite. As the spiciest of the three versions, the Roasted Hatch Chile and Cilantro Hummus appeals to those who want a bit more heat. To amp it up even more, roast an extra Hatch chile to chop and sprinkle atop the finished hummus. If you're making all three, save a step by roasting the red bell pepper alongside the Hatch chiles.

Makes about 2 cups hummus :: **V • Gluten-Free Option**

¼ cup tahini (sesame seed paste)

3 tablespoons freshly squeezed lemon juice

3 tablespoons extra-virgin olive oil, plus additional for serving

1 garlic clove, peeled (only if using canned beans)

¼ to ½ teaspoon kosher salt, plus additional to taste

1¾ cups drained Garlicky Garbanzo Beans (page 26), or 1 (15-ounce) can garbanzo beans, drained, some bean liquid reserved

Smoked paprika or regular paprika

Grilled flatbread, pita chips, or tortilla chips (gluten-free, if desired), and raw vegetables, for serving

---

BUILDING THE BEST HUMMUS

I've been making hummus for a couple of decades now, and I've read many theories (and tested a few) about what makes the best garbanzo bean dip. Some traditional cooks insist that you have to peel the cooked garbanzo beans. While it's a little less tedious than it sounds—squeeze gently and they pop right out of their skins—I have not found that particular task to be worth the effort. Others say the order in which you purée the ingredients is key, and I'll admit that the fluffiness that results from blending tahini, lemon juice, and olive oil together first is pretty convincing. But the most important thing for those who like a smooth, almost whipped texture is to use a powerful food processor. It also helps to prepare your beans from scratch: The Garlicky Garbanzo Beans recipe (page 26) provides enough beans for all three hummus variations in this book (page 25), making it a perfect place to start if you're cooking for a party. Extra beans freeze well: Pack them in an airtight container with some of the cooking water, seal, and freeze until needed.

Place the tahini and lemon juice in a food processor and blend well. Add the olive oil, raw garlic (if using), and salt. Blend well. Add the Garlicky Garbanzo Beans (including a few cooked garlic cloves from the pot) to the food processor and blend until smooth.

Thin to the desired consistency, if necessary, with a tablespoon or two of bean cooking liquid (from the pot if using homemade, or from the can). Season to taste with additional salt, if desired. Transfer the hummus to a shallow serving bowl, drizzle with additional olive oil, and sprinkle with paprika. Serve with grilled flatbread, pita chips, or tortilla chips, and raw vegetables.

Roasted Red Pepper Hummus: Preheat the broiler. Arrange an oven rack in the top third of the oven. Line a baking sheet with a sheet of foil. Place one red bell pepper on the foil and broil until the skin is blistered and blackening, turning once with tongs, 5 to 7 minutes per side. (If the pepper is very large, you might need to turn it to a third or fourth side to make sure the skin on all sides is blistering.) Remove the baking sheet from the oven, gather the foil around the pepper, and pinch the ends of the foil together to seal; let the peppers steam until the skin pulls off easily, about 15 minutes. Remove as much of the pepper's skin as possible. Seed and coarsely chop the pepper. Prepare the Classic Hummus recipe, adding the roasted red pepper plus 1 tablespoon of sriracha to the ingredients in the food processor, blending well. Season to taste with additional salt and sriracha.

Roasted Hatch Chile and Cilantro Hummus: Prepare four to five roasted Hatch or Anaheim chiles, steaming them and removing as much of the skin as possible (see Roasted Red Pepper Hummus instructions). Seed and coarsely chop the chiles (if you are using a fifth chile, finely chop it and reserve it as a topping for the finished hummus). Prepare the Classic Hummus, adding ⅔ cup of roasted chopped chiles plus ⅓ cup of loosely packed fresh cilantro leaves, blending well. Season to taste with additional salt, and top with the fifth chile, if using.

Garlicky Garbanzo Beans

This is the same brine-soak method I use for pinto beans. This recipe makes enough garbanzos to produce all three variations of hummus (see page 24), a great trio for entertaining. These fragrant, perfectly cooked garbanzos also are a welcome addition to cold salads or warm vegetable stews; they'd be wonderful in the Ratatouille with Creamy Polenta (page 94).

Makes about 6 cups beans :: **V • GF**

1 pound dried garbanzo beans

2 tablespoons kosher salt

1 large head of garlic, cloves separated and peeled

Place the beans in a colander and rinse well, picking out any that are shriveled or otherwise unappetizing.

Place the beans in a large pot. Add 8 cups of water and stir in the salt; soak the beans for at least 8 hours and up to 24 hours.

Pour the beans into the colander to drain, and rinse well. Return the beans to the pot and add 6 cups of water and the garlic cloves.

Cover and bring to a boil over medium-high heat. Lower the heat to low, cover, and simmer, stirring occasionally, until the beans are tender, 45 minutes to 1 hour longer (cooking time will vary depending on soaking time and freshness of the beans).

Spicy Pimiento Cheese with Pecans

Pimiento cheese sandwiches are one of the few meatless Southern staples available at most lunch spots—no substitutes necessary. Pimiento cheese also is great served on crackers as a snack, as it is here. Like things spicy? Add some extra sriracha to the mix.

Makes about 2 cups pimiento cheese :: **Gluten-Free Option**

8 ounces white Cheddar cheese, grated (about 2¾ cups loosely packed)

½ cup pecan halves, lightly toasted and chopped

¼ cup drained pimientos, finely chopped

2 green onions, thinly sliced (use the white and pale green parts, and about 1 inch of the dark green part to equal about 2 tablespoons total)

¼ cup plus 2 tablespoons mayonnaise

1½ teaspoons sriracha

Rice crackers (gluten-free, if desired), other crackers, or Grilled Multigrain Crostini (page 41), for serving

Place the cheese, pecans, pimientos, and green onions in a medium bowl; using your hands, toss the ingredients gently to combine.

In a small bowl, whisk the mayonnaise and sriracha to blend. Pour the mayonnaise mixture over the cheese mixture and stir gently with a fork until incorporated.

Cover and refrigerate for at least 2 hours to allow the flavors to develop. Serve chilled with crackers or crostini.

Can be prepared up to 2 days ahead. Cover and keep refrigerated.

Roasted Mixed Nuts with Rosemary

This little recipe is so simple and so much more than the sum of its parts. If you really want to show off, serve these nuts warm from the oven with a glass of sparkling wine. Rosemary provides for the Texas cook year-round or nearly year-round. I buy raw nuts and pepitas from the bulk bins at my local market; be sure to store them in the freezer because they go rancid quickly.

Makes about 2 cups nuts :: **V • GF**

½ cup raw cashews (about 2½ ounces)

½ cup raw walnut pieces (about 2 ounces)

½ cup raw pecan halves (about 2 ounces)

½ cup raw pepitas (about 2¼ ounces)

1 tablespoon extra-virgin olive oil

1 tablespoon chopped fresh rosemary

½ teaspoon kosher salt

Preheat the oven to 350°F. Spread out all the nuts and the pepitas in a 13 x 9 x 2-inch baking dish. Bake until lightly toasted, 10 to 12 minutes. Remove from the oven.

In a small bowl, whisk together the olive oil, rosemary, and salt. Pour the mixture over the hot nuts in the baking dish; using a rubber spatula, fold in the rosemary mixture until it is evenly distributed among the nuts. Transfer the nuts to a serving bowl. Serve warm or at room temperature.

Creamy Mushroom Pita Triangles

Anthony's wife, Michele, first made this appetizer for a dinner party they threw when they lived in Los Angeles. Ever since moving to Texas, he always suggests this dish for any gathering—big or small—because the mushroom triangles are irresistibly savory, creamy, and crispy. Michele prepares the mushrooms in two skillets to avoid crowding the pan, allowing for better browning. For smaller groups, prepare half the recipe, using just one pan. She serves this with the thin, crispy pita wedges here, but for thicker, chewier bread you can use the Grilled Multigrain Crostini recipe (page 41) instead.

Serves 8 to 10

6 ounces (1½ sticks) butter

1½ cups chopped shallots (from about 5 large shallots)

3 pounds cremini mushrooms, stems trimmed, sliced

¾ cup sweet Marsala

2 cups heavy whipping cream

¾ cup loosely packed fresh flat-leaf parsley leaves, chopped

1 (12- to 15-ounce) package pita bread, each round cut into six wedges (30 to 36 pieces)

Extra-virgin olive oil

Divide the butter between two very large, heavy skillets and melt it over medium-high heat.

Divide the shallots equally between the two skillets and sauté until the shallots begin to soften, 4 to 5 minutes.

Divide the mushrooms equally between the two skillets and sauté until the mushrooms are almost tender, about 8 minutes.

Add equal amounts of Marsala to both skillets; stir for 1 minute, or until the Marsala evaporates. Pour 1 cup of the cream into each skillet and cook until the sauce thickens, stirring occasionally, about 4 minutes. Remove from the heat.

Transfer the creamy mushroom mixture into one skillet to combine; stir in the parsley. Season generously to taste with salt and pepper.

The creamy mushroom mixture can be made 1 day ahead; let cool, then cover and refrigerate. Rewarm over medium heat, thinning with more cream, if necessary, before serving.

Preheat the oven to 350°F. Line a baking sheet with parchment paper or foil. Arrange the pita wedges in a single layer on the sheet. Brush the top of each pita wedge with olive oil. Bake until crisp, 9 to 10 minutes.

Spoon the warm mushroom mixture atop each pita wedge and serve.

Lemony Deviled Eggs with Spring Herbs

This version of the old-school finger food features bright-tasting chives and cilantro; feel free to swap those out for whatever tender spring herbs you might have on hand—flat-leaf parsley and dill also would be nice.

Makes 12 filled egg halves :: **GF**

6 large eggs

2 tablespoons mayonnaise

2 tablespoons sour cream

¼ cup loosely packed fresh cilantro leaves

1 small garlic clove, peeled

Zest from 1 lemon (about 1 teaspoon)

1 tablespoon chopped fresh chives

1 tablespoon freshly squeezed lemon juice

½ teaspoon dry mustard (optional)

¼ teaspoon kosher salt

Smoked paprika for garnish (optional)

Place the eggs in a pot, add enough water to fully submerge them, cover the pot, and bring to a boil.

When the water reaches a boil, turn off the heat immediately, and let the eggs stand, covered, for 20 minutes. Meanwhile, fill a large bowl with ice water. Using a slotted spoon, transfer the cooked eggs to the ice water to cool for 10 minutes.

Remove the shells and halve each egg lengthwise, transferring the cooked yolks to a small bowl and placing the egg whites, rounded side down, on a small serving platter.

Add the mayonnaise and sour cream to the cooked egg yolks and mash with a fork. Finely mince the cilantro, garlic, and lemon zest, and add to the mixture. Next, add the chives, lemon juice, mustard, if desired, and salt.

Mash the mixture well with a fork, leaving it as chunky or making it as smooth as you like. Using a rubber spatula, spoon the mixture into a resealable plastic sandwich bag, snip off one end, and pipe the filling evenly into the twelve egg white halves. Sprinkle with the smoked paprika, if desired, and serve.

Can be prepared up to a day ahead of time. Cover and refrigerate.

Natural Cheddar and Jack Queso

The queso many people crave is made with Velveeta, and it's pretty easy snacking if you don't think about what's in it. I have never purchased Velveeta, and, not having arrived in Texas until my thirties, I have no plans to start. In the years since I landed in the Lone Star State, I've tried making several versions of Velveeta-free queso. I had high hopes for one made fondue-style, only with beer instead of wine (it was delicious on the stove but didn't stay smooth and creamy when cooler). So I took a tip from the Homesick Texan blog and started instead with a white sauce—cornstarch here keeps the roux gluten-free—and found it makes for a surprisingly stable base; it can even be refrigerated and zapped to enjoy again later. Serve warm ladled over tortilla chips, if only once in a while.

Makes about 3 cups queso :: **GF**

1 (10-ounce can) original or Mexican Ro*Tel diced tomatoes and green chiles

2 tablespoons unsalted butter

2 small garlic cloves, peeled and minced

2 tablespoons cornstarch

1 cup whole milk

8 ounces Monterey Jack cheese, grated

8 ounces sharp Cheddar cheese, grated

½ cup loosely packed fresh cilantro leaves, chopped, plus additional cilantro leaves for garnish

Tortilla chips (gluten-free, if desired), for serving

Pour the Ro*Tel into a colander to drain.

Melt the butter in a medium, heavy saucepan over medium-low heat. Add the garlic and stir for 30 seconds. Add the cornstarch and whisk until smooth and bubbling, allowing the roux to bubble for about 2 minutes (it should not brown).

Add the milk and whisk until the mixture bubbles and thickens, about 3 minutes. Add the drained Ro*Tel and whisk until heated through, about 2 minutes.

Add the cheeses one handful at a time, whisking gently until melted and incorporated before adding the next handful. After all the cheese is incorporated, whisk in the cilantro.

Arrange the tortilla chips on a large platter; ladle the warm queso generously over the chips, sprinkle with additional cilantro leaves to garnish, and serve immediately.

Any leftover queso can be allowed to cool, then covered and refrigerated. Rewarm the queso on the stovetop or in the microwave, stirring occasionally.

Nachos with Refried Beans

There are two camps on nachos: piled high and messy or baked neatly in a single layer. It's your call. If you plan to top and bake individual nachos, choose tortilla chips that are large and sturdy instead of the thinner restaurant-style ones.

Makes about 4 servings; doubles easily :: **GF**

About 20 large, sturdy tortilla chips, or ½ (12- to 13-ounce) package standard-size tortilla chips (gluten-free, if desired)

1½ cups Refried Beans (page 35), or 1 (16-ounce) can vegetarian refried beans

4 ounces sharp Cheddar cheese, grated (about 1 cup packed)

1 jalapeño pepper, very thinly sliced into rounds (seeds left in), or 20 pickled jalapeño slices

Sour cream, for serving (optional)

Salsa, such as Restaurant-Style Smoky Red Salsa (page 23), for serving (optional)

Preheat the oven to 350°F. Line a baking sheet with parchment paper. Spread the large tortilla chips out on the baking sheet in a single layer. (Alternatively, pour the tortilla chips into an 8-inch square baking dish or other 2-quart baking dish.)

Warm the refried beans in a small, heavy saucepan over medium heat, stirring occasionally.

Using a rubber spatula, divide the warmed refried beans equally among the chips, and spread them atop each chip. (Or, if using a baking dish instead, spoon the warm refried beans evenly atop the chips, leaving a 1-inch border of untopped chips around the edge.)

Sprinkle the beans with shredded cheese. Top each nacho with one slice of jalapeño (or sprinkle the jalapeños evenly over the cheese in the baking dish). Bake until the cheese is melted and bubbling, 10 to 15 minutes.

Serve warm, passing the sour cream and salsa separately, if desired.

Refried Beans

Mashed-up pintos are another on the long list of restaurant dishes that could so easily be vegetarian but often aren't (they're traditionally prepared with lard or sometimes bacon grease). That's why, when out and about, I usually order black beans. The truth is, I far prefer pintos—especially when they're prepared at home from scratch, and even more so when they're made into refried beans. Use these refried beans on nachos (see page 34), in burritos, or as a simple side dish.

Makes about 3½ cups beans :: **V • GF**

¼ cup canola oil or olive oil

1 cup finely diced yellow onion (from about ½ medium-size onion)

4 garlic cloves (skip if using Garlicky Pinto Beans), peeled and minced

1 teaspoon chili powder, or more to taste

½ teaspoon smoked paprika

3½ cups prepared Garlicky Pinto Beans (page 76), or 2 (15-ounce) cans pinto beans, drained and rinsed

Salt

Heat the oil in a medium, heavy skillet over medium-high heat.

Add the onion and sauté until translucent and tender, about 3 minutes. Add the garlic, if using, and sauté for 1 minute longer. Stir in the chili powder and paprika. Stir in the drained beans (include a couple of garlic cloves from the pot if using Garlicky Pinto Beans).

Using a handheld potato masher or a wire pastry blender, coarsely mash the beans in the skillet, making the mixture as smooth or chunky as you like.

Stir the mashed beans until they are hot all the way through. Thin the beans with a tablespoon or two of the bean-cooking liquid or water, if desired, and adjust the seasoning to taste with salt and additional chili powder, if desired. Serve warm.

Greener Goddess Dip with Fresh Vegetables

A great vegetable platter is a must-have for every cook's repertoire. I put this out for parties, of course, but I also frequently make a quick veggie platter to hold off hungry kids while I'm cooking a meal. (Bonus: They will have eaten at least a serving of vegetables before we even sit down for dinner.) The old-fashioned dip is fabulous made with a generous helping of ripe avocado; use vegan mayonnaise (such as Vegenaise) for a purely plant-based version. Serve it with fresh raw veggies, such as red, orange, and yellow bell peppers, carrots, and bite-size tomatoes, plus crisp-tender, lightly steamed sugar snap peas or asparagus. It's also great with potato chips.

Makes about 1 cup dip : : **Vegan Option • GF**

1 small, ripe avocado

½ cup loosely packed fresh flat-leaf parsley leaves

½ cup mayonnaise or vegan mayonnaise (such as Vegenaise)

3 green onions, thinly sliced (use white, pale green, and up to 2 inches of dark green part to make about ¼ cup total)

2 tablespoons freshly squeezed lemon juice, or more to taste

1 garlic clove, peeled, smashed, and coarsely chopped

1 teaspoon seasoned rice vinegar

½ teaspoon dried tarragon

¼ teaspoon kosher salt, or more to taste

Fresh raw or lightly steamed vegetables, such as carrot sticks, bell pepper slices, steamed sugar snap peas, or steamed asparagus stalks, for serving (see page 37 for tips on steaming vegetables)

Halve and pit the avocado; squeeze the avocado flesh into a blender or food processor.

Add the flat-leaf parsley, mayonnaise or vegan mayonnaise, green onions, lemon juice, 2 tablespoons of water, and the garlic, rice vinegar, tarragon, and salt. Blend until completely puréed.

Adjust the seasoning to taste with additional lemon juice and salt, if necessary. Serve chilled with your choice of raw or steamed vegetables.

The dip can be prepared up to 1 day ahead. Cover and keep refrigerated.

STEAMING YOUR WAY TO CRISP-TENDER

Steaming has a reputation for being the boring cooking method of the diet-conscious. But for certain vegetables, I've found that it's the surest technique for achieving that perfect balance between crisp and tender, bringing out a green vegetable's brightest color and flavor. (Green vegetables should never, ever be overcooked; I'm absolutely convinced that our tendency to overcook vegetables is why so many people think they don't like them.) Steaming works wonders with asparagus and sugar snap peas. Fit a steamer or pasta insert into a large pot (if you don't have one, place a metal colander atop a soup pot). Then, fill the pot with an inch or two of water (the water should not touch the bottom of the steamer) and bring it to a boil. Place the green vegetables in the steamer insert, cover, and cook until bright green and crisp-tender, about 5 minutes for asparagus or sugar snap peas. Rinse the vegetables immediately with cold water to stop the cooking, then chill them until ready to serve; try them with the Greener Goddess Dip (page 36).

Big Ol' Antipasto Platter

This dish is a cocktail party on a plate (well, the food part of the party, anyway—see page 205 for the drinks). This big spread of roasted peppers, mushrooms, artichoke hearts, olives, and cheese just needs a side of crostini as a vehicle for all the colors, flavors, and textures on offer. While it's easy to roast the peppers at home, if you're in a big hurry, you can purchase roasted ones from the market. For a vegan platter, swap out the cheese for some roasted bite-size tomatoes. McPherson's ample and vibrant Chenin Blanc is a perfect white wine for the platter.

Makes about 10 servings

Peppers and Mushrooms

1 large red bell pepper

1 large yellow bell pepper

1 large orange bell pepper

8 ounces fresh cremini or button mushrooms, trimmed and halved

2 tablespoons extra-virgin olive oil

1 teaspoon chopped fresh rosemary

¼ teaspoon kosher salt

⅛ teaspoon freshly ground black pepper

Vinaigrette

¼ cup plus 1 tablespoon extra-virgin olive oil

2 tablespoons freshly squeezed lemon juice

2 teaspoons seasoned rice vinegar

¼ teaspoon kosher salt

⅛ teaspoon freshly ground black pepper

2 tablespoons chopped fresh flat-leaf parsley

1 tablespoon chopped fresh chives

Assembly

1 (14-ounce) can artichokes hearts in brine, drained and halved or quartered lengthwise

1¾ cups pitted green or black olives (about 6 ounces)

1 (8-ounce) container *ciliegine* (small fresh mozzarella balls), or 1 (8- to 11-ounce) log soft, fresh goat cheese, sliced (optional)

RECIPE CONTINUES

To broil the peppers and mushrooms: Preheat the broiler. Arrange an oven rack in the top third of the oven.

Line a baking sheet with a large sheet of foil. Place the three peppers on the foil and broil until the skin is blistered and blackening, turning once with tongs, 5 to 7 minutes per side. (If the peppers are very large, you might need to turn them to a third or fourth side to make sure the skin on all sides is blistering.)

Remove the baking sheet from the oven, gather the foil around the peppers, and pinch the ends of the foil together to seal; let the peppers steam until the skin pulls off easily, about 15 minutes. Remove as much of the peppers' skin as possible. Rinse the peppers, removing the seeds. Transfer the peppers to a cutting board and slice them into ½-inch-wide strips. Place the peppers in a colander over a bowl or the sink to drain off any excess liquid.

Lower the oven temperature to 450°F and move the oven rack back down to the middle of the oven.

In a medium bowl, whisk the olive oil with the rosemary, salt, and black pepper. Add the mushroom halves and toss to coat.

Line a medium baking dish with parchment paper and arrange the coated mushrooms in a single layer in the dish. Roast the mushrooms until they are cooked through, somewhat shriveled, and just beginning to brown in spots, stirring occasionally, 20 to 25 minutes. Let cool.

For the vinaigrette: In a small bowl or glass measuring cup, whisk the olive oil, lemon juice, vinegar, salt, and pepper to blend. Whisk in the parsley and chives. Set aside.

To assemble: On a large serving platter, arrange the roasted pepper strips, mushrooms, artichoke hearts, olives, and cheese, if using. Rewhisk the vinaigrette and, using a spoon, drizzle it over the ingredients, zigzagging across all of them. Cover with plastic wrap and refrigerate until ready to serve. Can be prepared up to a day or two ahead of time.

Grilled Multigrain Crostini

These little toasts are more than the sum of their parts, and solid enough to stand up to generous amounts of toppings; try them with the Big Ol' Antipasto Platter (page 39), or the Spicy Pimiento Cheese with Pecans (page 27). I usually use a multigrain baguette, but feel free to use any favorite bread; grilled flatbread makes a great accompaniment for hummus. If you have the grill going already, go that route—it gives them extra smokiness and a crisp but not dry texture. Otherwise, follow the instructions for toasting these in the oven.

Makes about 3 dozen crostini :: **V**

1 (11.5-ounce) multigrain baguette, or 1 whole wheat
    or traditional baguette (vegan, if desired)

¼ cup extra-virgin olive oil

Kosher salt

Freshly ground black pepper

To grill

Preheat the grill to medium-high (about 375°F). Place a perforated stainless-steel grill topper on the counter. Slice the baguette on the diagonal into ½-inch-thick slices. Arrange the baguette slices on the prepared pan. Pour the olive oil into a small bowl. Using a pastry brush, lightly brush each baguette slice on both sides with the olive oil. Sprinkle the tops of the baguette slices lightly with kosher salt and freshly ground black pepper. Grill the baguette slices until they are lightly toasted and just beginning to darken around the edges, turning once, about 2 minutes per side. Serve warm or at room temperature.

To bake

Preheat the oven to 350°F. Line a baking sheet with parchment paper. Slice the baguette on the diagonal into ½-inch-thick slices. Arrange the baguette slices on the prepared baking sheet. Pour the olive oil into a small bowl. Using a pastry brush, lightly brush each baguette slice on both sides with the olive oil. Sprinkle the tops of the baguette slices lightly with kosher salt and freshly ground black pepper. Bake the baguette slices until they are lightly toasted and just beginning to brown around the edges, 10 to 15 minutes. Serve warm or at room temperature.

Chisholm Trail Mix

My husband, Till, often makes a trail mix to take with us, whether we're actually hitting the trail—hiking, biking, or camping—or just hitting the interstate for a road trip. His name for this mix refers to a new parkway in Fort Worth as well as the historic cattle-drive route from Texas to Kansas; our trips might be far less grueling, but I am always so grateful for a handful of this mix halfway through a long hike or after a few hours on the road. While we both like salted roasted nuts with drinks at home, on the go, raw nuts deliver energy without all the thirst-inducing sodium. Visit the bulk bins at your closest natural foods market and customize it to your tastes.

Makes about 4 cups trail mix :: **Vegan Option • GF**

½ heaping cup bittersweet chocolate chips (vegan, if desired); for hot weather, dark-chocolate M&Ms

½ cup coarsely broken raw walnut pieces

½ cup roasted unsalted peanuts

½ cup whole raw almonds

½ cup raw pepitas or sunflower seeds

½ cup coarsely broken banana chips

½ cup diced dried apricots or mangoes

½ cup dried sweetened cranberries or raisins

½ cup sweetened shredded coconut

Combine all the ingredients in an airtight container or a resealable plastic bag. Cover or seal and shake gently.

Can be prepared up to 3 days ahead. Keep sealed airtight at room temperature, or in a cooler.

Grilled Edamame

Sure, you can just boil these young, tender soybeans in salty water and leave it at that, but a sprinkle of spice and a turn over the fire gives this favorite snack a nice smoky touch.

Makes about 4 servings :: **V • GF**

1 (14- to 16-ounce) bag frozen edamame in pods

2 tablespoons canola oil

½ teaspoon kosher salt

½ teaspoon garlic powder (gluten-free, if desired)

⅛ teaspoon cayenne pepper

Preheat the grill to medium-high (375°F). Place a large perforated stainless-steel grill topper atop the grill grate.

Bring a medium pot of salted water to a boil. Add the edamame to the water, cover, and cook for 5 minutes (the water should return to a boil). Pour the edamame into a colander to drain; rinse with cold water to stop the cooking.

In a large bowl, whisk the oil with the salt, garlic powder, and cayenne. Add the drained edamame to the bowl. Using your hands, toss the edamame to coat with the spice mixture.

Pour the edamame onto the hot grill pan and spread them out in a single layer as much as possible. Grill the edamame just until the pods begin to brown in spots, stirring around and turning the pods over once, 7 to 8 minutes total.

Transfer the edamame to a serving platter and serve warm or at room temperature.

Sautéed Okra with Lemon-Chive Aïoli

Okra is abundant at local farmers' markets and grows well in Texas backyards; it's especially popular pickled or breaded and fried. At home I opt for a simple sautéed version—this is the time to pull out your cast-iron skillet to get those deliciously browned spots on the outside of the okra, while keeping the inside crisp-tender. Garlicky mayonnaise, also known as aïoli, makes a simple dipping sauce; try the Lemon-Chive Aïoli (page 45) or the Cilantro-Chili Aïoli (page 169).

Makes about 4 servings :: **Vegan Option • GF**

Lemon-Chive Aïoli (page 45)

1 tablespoon extra-virgin olive oil

8 ounces fresh okra, stem ends trimmed

Kosher salt

Freshly ground black pepper

Place the aïoli in a small bowl. Can be prepared up to a day ahead. Cover and refrigerate until ready to prepare the okra.

Just before serving, heat the oil in a large, heavy cast-iron skillet over medium-high heat (the skillet should be very hot before adding the okra). Add the okra and sauté until bright green and beginning to brown in spots, 5 to 6 minutes. Transfer the okra to a small serving platter. Season to taste with salt and pepper. Place the bowl of aïoli on the same serving platter and serve the okra warm.

Lemon-Chive Aïoli

Aïoli can be used as a sauce, spread, or dip. Flavored aioli is easy to make with purchased mayonnaise or vegan mayonnaise (such as Vegenaise, one of the commercially prepared vegan stand-ins that I love). Aïoli really shines when served with sautéed okra (see page 44), or steamed asparagus or sugar snap peas (see sidebar, page 37).

Makes about ½ cup aïoli :: **Vegan Option • GF**

½ cup mayonnaise or vegan mayonnaise (such as Vegenaise)

1 tablespoon chopped fresh chives

2 teaspoons freshly squeezed lemon juice

1 small garlic clove, minced

Salt (optional)

Pepper (optional)

Combine the mayonnaise or vegan mayonnaise, chives, lemon juice, and garlic in a small bowl and whisk to blend well. Season to taste with salt and pepper, if desired. Can be prepared up to a day ahead of time. Cover with plastic wrap and refrigerate.

SOUPS & SALADS

Vegetarians, you see, are supposed to eat lots and lots of . . . salad. But the average bowl of lightly dressed greens—too often an afterthought—isn't hotly anticipated so much as it is dutifully eaten. Homemade salad dressings make a big difference, and the right greens set the tone, too: A mix of baby spinach, kale, and chard has a hearty and wholesome texture, while baby spring or herb mixes are tender and flavorful. Add grilled portobello strips or a nut-crusted goat cheese round and you'll have a salad to swoon over. Making soup from scratch is always worth the effort; as well as being thrifty and nourishing, homemade soups are more vibrant (and less salty) than their store-bought counterparts. Homemade soup served with panini is a favorite light supper at my house, popular with the grown-ups and kids alike.

Buck Up Vegetarian Vegetable Soup

Do you know when you need a pot of homemade soup the most? When you're sick—and that, sadly, is when you will least feel like cooking anything from scratch. I bring you this simple soup recipe for exactly those days. It makes shameless use of frozen veggies and canned goods, leaving only three things to chop—and it will create a big enough pot of soup to enjoy for several days running, enough to eat until you feel better (leftovers also freeze beautifully). Use purchased vegetable stock, vegetable bouillon cubes dissolved in boiling water, or just water. If you have Creole seasoning (my Louisiana friends have gotten me on to the Tony Chachere's brand), use it in place of the cayenne, salt, and pepper. My family loves this soup with grilled cheese sandwiches.

Makes about 12 servings :: **V • GF**

2 tablespoons olive oil

1 large yellow or white onion, finely chopped

1½ pounds Yukon Gold potatoes (4 medium-size to large), scrubbed and chopped into ½-inch pieces

8 ounces carrots (about 4 medium-size), peeled and thinly sliced into rounds no more than ¼ inch thick

4 garlic cloves, peeled and minced

4 cups vegetable stock (vegan, if desired)

1 (28-ounce) can or 2 (14.5-ounce) cans fire-roasted crushed or fire-roasted chopped tomatoes

2 cups frozen or fresh white corn kernels

2 cups frozen lima beans

1 (15- to 16-ounce) can pinto beans, drained

½ teaspoon kosher salt, or more to taste

¼ teaspoon cayenne pepper, or more to taste

¼ teaspoon freshly ground black pepper, or more to taste

Heat the olive oil in a large pot over medium-high heat.

Add the onion and sauté until soft and translucent, about 5 minutes.

Add the potatoes, carrots, and garlic; cook, stirring, for 3 minutes.

Add the stock plus 4 cups of water, and the tomatoes, corn, lima beans, and pinto beans. Bring to a boil. Lower the heat to medium-low and simmer, covered, until the potatoes and carrots are tender, 25 to 30 minutes.

Stir in the salt, cayenne, and black pepper. Season to taste with additional salt, cayenne pepper, and black pepper, if desired. Serve warm.

Baked Tofu, Pine Nut, and Cilantro Salad

This recipe comes from Michele Head, who has made it and enjoyed it with friends countless times. It's unusual, but it's very quick and easy to make, thanks to the convenience of preseasoned, prebaked tofu. It'll stand in for a light lunch with a slice of crusty bread, or serve it alongside an Asian-inspired dinner with a glass of Sauvignon Blanc.

Makes 4 servings : : **V • GF**

⅓ cup pine nuts

1 large bunch (about 5 ounces) fresh organic cilantro (you'll need both the leaves and the stems)

½ to 1 whole (7- to 8-ounce) container five-spice or teriyaki-flavored baked tofu (gluten-free, if desired), chopped into ¼-inch cubes

1 tablespoon organic granulated sugar

2 teaspoons seasoned rice vinegar

1½ teaspoons toasted sesame oil

¼ to ½ teaspoon sea salt

Heat the pine nuts in a dry skillet over medium heat until they just start to turn golden, about 3 minutes; set aside.

Wash the cilantro and trim off the very ends of the stems (you'll need most of the stems for the salad). Fill a medium bowl with cold water, adding a couple of ice cubes, and set aside. Fill a large pot half-full with salted water, cover, and bring to a boil; add the cilantro and boil for 10 seconds. Drain and immediately place the cilantro in the bowl of cold water to stop the cooking. Drain the cilantro again and squeeze dry. Chop the cilantro into roughly ½-inch lengths and place it in a salad bowl. Add the tofu, using at least half of the package and up to the whole package, depending on the ratio of tofu to cilantro desired. Add the pine nuts.

In a small bowl, whisk the sugar, vinegar, sesame oil, and salt to blend. Add it to the cilantro mixture and toss to combine. Can be prepared up to a day ahead. Cover and refrigerate.

Barley and Spinach Salad with Lemon-Mustard Dressing

If you haven't cooked with pearl barley before, give it a try; it's got a terrific toothsome texture and is perfectly suited for using in this chilled salad. While this recipe makes a great side dish for a cookout or potluck, bringing far more flavor and nutrition to the table than does a typical potato or pasta salad, it's also a great meatless lunch to take to the office.

Makes about 6 servings :: **Vegan Option**

¾ cup dried pearl barley, rinsed

1 cup dried green lentils, rinsed

2 cups packed (2½ to 3 ounces) fresh baby spinach leaves, thinly sliced

2 tablespoons minced shallot (from about 1 large shallot)

¼ cup extra-virgin olive oil

2 tablespoons freshly squeezed lemon juice

2 tablespoons seasoned rice vinegar

2 teaspoons Dijon mustard

1 small garlic clove, peeled, crushed, and minced

½ teaspoon kosher salt

½ cup queso fresco, crumbled soft fresh goat cheese, or feta cheese (optional; omit for vegan)

In a medium, heavy saucepan, combine the barley with 2¼ cups of water and a pinch of salt. Cover and bring to a boil. Lower the heat to medium-low and simmer, covered, until the water is absorbed and the barley is tender, about 45 minutes. Transfer the cooked barley to a large mixing bowl and allow it to cool.

Bring a medium, heavy saucepan of salted water to a boil. Stir in the lentils, cover, and return the water to a boil. Lower the heat to medium-low and simmer, covered, stirring occasionally, until the lentils are tender, about 20 minutes. Drain the lentils in a colander and rinse with cold water to stop the cooking. Add the cooked lentils to the barley.

Add the sliced spinach and shallot to the barley mixture and toss gently to combine.

In a small bowl, combine the oil, lemon juice, vinegar, mustard, garlic, and salt. Whisk to blend well. Drizzle the dressing over the salad and toss gently to coat.

Add the crumbled cheese, if using, and toss gently. Cover and refrigerate until ready to serve. Can be prepared 1 day ahead of time. Keep chilled.

Pastry-Topped Butternut Squash Soup with Apples and Thyme

///

Nobody would suspect that this creamy soup with a pastry top actually is vegan (Pepperidge Farm Puff Pastry is free of dairy and eggs). While that doesn't necessarily make the pastry part healthful, it does make it a fun, special-occasion topping that nearly everyone can enjoy. Without the pastry, the soup is gluten-free, too. While short cooking times are best when it comes to green vegetables, for this soup it's critical that the squash, carrots, and apple cook until they're absolutely tender, almost falling apart. I often use vegetable bouillon instead of boxed or homemade vegetable stock, as it takes up so little room in the pantry, and certain varieties have very good flavor. (I like the Rapunzel brand Vegan Vegetable Bouillon with Sea Salt & Herbs.) A sharp new peeler makes short work of peeling butternut squash; if you find that to be too much trouble, halve and roast the squash until it's soft enough to be scooped out with a spoon.

Makes about 8 servings (about 12 cups) :: **V**

¼ cup extra-virgin olive oil

1 large sweet onion, coarsely chopped (about 3 cups)

2 large carrots, peeled and coarsely chopped (about 1½ cups)

1 large butternut squash, peeled, seeded, and coarsely chopped (about 6 cups)

2 medium-size crisp apples, such as Gala, peeled, cored, and coarsely chopped (about 3 cups)

1 teaspoon dried thyme leaves

6 cups vegetable stock (vegan, if desired)

1 (17.3-ounce) package frozen puff pastry sheets (such as Pepperidge Farm; vegan, if desired), thawed

Heat the olive oil in a large, heavy pot over medium-high heat.

Add the onion and carrots and sauté until the onions are translucent and tender, about 10 minutes. Add the butternut squash and sauté for 5 minutes longer. Add the apples and sprinkle with the thyme; sauté for another 5 minutes.

Add the stock, cover, and bring to boil. Lower the heat to low and simmer covered, stirring occasionally, until all the vegetables are very tender, 30 to 35 minutes. Remove from the heat.

Using a handheld immersion blender, blend the soup until the vegetables are completely puréed and the soup has a smooth texture (alternatively, working in batches, use a standing blender. filling it no more than half-full, to purée the soup, returning it to the pot before continuing). The soup can be prepared ahead of time. Let cool, then cover and refrigerate. Rewarm before serving.

To prepare the pastry topping: Preheat the oven to 400°F. Ladle the room-temperature or warm soup into ovenproof bowls, filling them no more than two-thirds full, and place the bowls on a baking sheet.

Unfold one sheet of thawed puff pastry onto a floured work surface. Cut the pastry sheet into four equal squares, and roll them out enough so that each pastry square is just large enough to cover one bowl. Repeat with second sheet of puff pastry for a total of eight squares.

Drape one pastry square atop each bowl of soup, pinching around edge of each bowl. Bake until the pastry is puffed and golden brown, 18 to 20 minutes. Let cool for 10 minutes before serving; serve warm.

Grapefruit and Avocado Salad with Pomegranate-Shallot Vinaigrette

Such light, bright fare is always a welcome change of pace in the wintertime, when Texas grapefruit comes into season. While Himalayan Pink sea salt sounds fancy, it's widely available (my current bottle is from Costco), and its fine texture and light flavor make it a great finishing salt. Otherwise, standard sea salt or kosher salt will do.

Makes about 4 servings; doubles easily :: **V • GF**

½ large shallot, minced (about 2 tablespoons)

2 tablespoons extra-virgin olive oil

1 tablespoon pomegranate or raspberry vinegar

½ teaspoon Dijon mustard

½ large (12-ounce) head Boston or Bibb lettuce, washed, drained, and torn into bite-size pieces

1 large avocado, peeled, pitted, and sliced into ⅓-inch-thick slices

1 large Ruby Red grapefruit

Himalayan Pink sea salt (optional)

In a small bowl, whisk the shallot, olive oil, vinegar, and mustard to blend.

Arrange the lettuce on a large platter. Top with the avocado slices. Cut the peel and pith away from the grapefruit and section the fruit, arranging the sections atop the salad. Squeeze the grapefruit core to extract the remaining juice, sprinkling over the salad.

Drizzle as much of the vinaigrette over the salad as desired. Sprinkle the salad lightly with sea salt, if desired, and serve. Can be prepared up to 2 hours ahead of time. Cover and refrigerate. Serve chilled.

WINE: Fall Creek Vineyards' Sauvignon Blanc is a tremendously versatile white wine that pairs beautifully with so many salads in this book. Here, it'll pick up on the grapefruit flavor and run with it.

BEER: Jester King's La Vie en Rose is a farmhouse ale refermented with raspberries. The sweet-tart flavors complement the tangy nature of the salad.

HOW TO SLICE A GRAPEFRUIT

Texans have good reason to be proud of our Ruby Red and Rio Star grapefruit. The big, red-fleshed citrus from South Texas starts showing up in our markets as early as October and stays all winter. We ship boxes of them off to friends at Christmastime; bring them along if we travel in the winter; offer them to houseguests at breakfast; and serve them alongside pastries on birthday mornings. While great on its own, the tart-sweet fruit also begs to be used in cocktail recipes, and it's a popular winter salad ingredient, too. Weighing upward of a pound apiece, these giants can be a little intimidating at first, but really, if you're not serving them the old-fashioned way (halved, with a serrated spoon), you can slice or section them just like an orange. Here's how it's done.

1. Using a sharp knife, slice off the stem end and the opposite end, forming flat surfaces that graze the grapefruit flesh on either end.

2. Place the grapefruit flat-side down on a work surface. Working from the top to the bottom, slice away all pith and peel, leaving the fruit exposed. Turn the grapefruit on its side. At this point, you may choose to slice it horizontally and serve it with the sections intact for a pretty, round presentation.

3. Or, for segments, slice just inside each grapefruit segment to separate the fruit from the pith, making two slices to release each.

Raw Zucchini Ribbon and Cherry Tomato Salad

So simple, so easy, and so elegant: A sharp vegetable peeler turns raw zucchini into a restaurant-style salad. Prepare this dish as close to serving time as possible because the zucchini releases water—and things get a little soupier after it sits.

Makes about 4 servings :: **V • GF**

2 tablespoons extra-virgin olive oil

1 tablespoon freshly squeezed lemon juice

1 teaspoon seasoned rice vinegar

¼ teaspoon kosher salt

1 pound (about 2 medium-size) zucchini

5 ounces (about 1 cup) assorted cherry tomatoes (use a variety of shapes and colors if you have them), halved

2 tablespoons minced shallot (from 1 small or ½ large)

1 tablespoon chopped fresh chives

Whisk the oil, lemon juice, vinegar, and salt in a small bowl to combine.

Trim the zucchini and place it on a cutting board. Working with a sharp vegetable peeler, slice lengthwise into thin ribbons, placing them in a colander as you work.

When ready to serve, transfer the zucchini ribbons to a bowl. Add the tomatoes and shallot. Add the vinaigrette and toss gently to coat. Garnish with the chives. Serve immediately.

Baby Greens Salad with Avocado and Creamy Tahini-Ginger Vinaigrette

This is especially pretty (and delicious) made with bite-size heirloom tomatoes in a variety of colors. Creamy avocado and toasted walnuts make this salad a hearty accompaniment for roasted vegetables or something off the grill.

Makes 4 to 6 servings :: **V • GF**

5 ounces (5 to 6 cups lightly packed) red and green baby romaine lettuce leaves or mixed baby greens, such as spinach, chard, and kale

6 to 8 ounces bite-size tomatoes, halved

1 medium-size avocado, peeled, pitted, and diced (about 6 ounces)

½ cup walnut pieces, lightly toasted

Creamy Tahini-Ginger Vinaigrette (page 59)

Pile the lettuce into a large salad bowl; top with the tomatoes, avocado, and walnut pieces.

Drizzle with just enough of the dressing to coat, tossing well. Serve, passing additional dressing separately.

Creamy Tahini-Ginger Vinaigrette

Don't have fresh ginger? Substituting garlic takes this in a deliciously different direction.

Makes about ½ cup dressing :: **V • GF**

¼ cup extra-virgin olive oil

2 tablespoons tahini (sesame seed paste)

2 tablespoons freshly squeezed lemon juice

1 tablespoon seasoned rice vinegar

2 teaspoons tamari

1 teaspoon agave nectar

1 tablespoon peeled and minced fresh ginger,
    or 1 small garlic clove, peeled and minced

Kosher salt

In a small bowl, whisk the olive oil, tahini, lemon juice, vinegar, tamari, agave nectar, and ginger to blend well. (For a smoother dressing, purée all the ingredients in a blender.) Season to taste with salt.

Can be prepared up to 2 days ahead. Cover and refrigerate. Bring to room temperature and rewhisk before using; note that the dressing thickens when cold.

Roasted Beet and Baby Greens Salad

This hearty winter salad could stand in as a light main course, especially if you top each serving with a round of Nut-Crusted Goat Cheese (page 65). Any color beets—red, golden, white, or even striped—will work; a mixture is especially pretty.

Makes 4 to 6 servings :: **Vegan Option • GF**

12 ounces fresh beets (3 to 4 medium-size beets), trimmed

1 tablespoon extra-virgin olive oil

¼ teaspoon kosher salt

5 ounces (5 to 6 cups lightly packed) mixed baby greens, such as spinach, chard, and kale

Creamy Honey-Dijon Dressing (page 62)

½ cup pecan or walnut pieces, lightly toasted and coarsely chopped

Preheat the oven to 400°F. Line a 13 x 9 x 2-inch baking dish with parchment paper.

Using a vegetable peeler, peel the beets. Cut the beets into ½-inch chunks; place them in a medium bowl. Drizzle with the olive oil and sprinkle with the salt; toss to coat.

Transfer the beets to the prepared baking dish. Roast until the beets are tender, stirring occasionally, 35 to 40 minutes. Let cool to room temperature.

Pile the greens into a large salad bowl; drizzle with enough of the dressing to coat, tossing well. Top the salad with the roasted beets, and sprinkle it with the toasted nuts. Serve, passing additional dressing separately.

Creamy Honey-Dijon Dressing

This easy rendition of honey-mustard comes together in minutes and may be prepared with agave nectar instead of honey, if you like; use it on any green salad.

Makes about ½ cup dressing :: **Vegan Option • GF**

¼ cup extra-virgin olive oil

2 tablespoons local honey or (for vegan) agave nectar

2 tablespoons freshly squeezed lemon juice

1 tablespoon Dijon or yellow mustard

1 tablespoon mayonnaise or vegan mayonnaise (such as Vegenaise)

⅛ to ¼ teaspoon kosher salt

⅛ teaspoon freshly ground black pepper

In a small bowl, combine all the ingredients and whisk to blend well.

Alternatively, combine all the ingredients in a small jar with a lid, cover, and shake well to blend. Can be prepared up to 3 days ahead. Store in an airtight container in the refrigerator. Rewhisk or shake before using.

ROUND ROCK HONEY

Here in Texas, the local honey is infused with subtle flavors collected from our own varied and unique landscape (think wildflowers, sage, mesquite). Austin-based Round Rock Honey, run by Konrad and Elizabeth Bouffard, has roughly ninety sites where the company tends biodynamic hives and "robs" only a frame or two at a time from each, sharing the spoils with the bees to maintain healthy hives. (Round Rock Honey also offers three-hour beginning beekeeping workshops that are pretty fascinating.) The resulting raw, unfiltered honey is deep amber in color and rich in flavor, more floral and subtly sweet than what you might find in a typical honey bear. One of my favorite ways to use honey is atop warm whole-grain toast spread with crunchy almond butter. It makes a brilliant sweet-salty contrast when drizzled over cheese, and it's soothing to the throat when stirred into hot tea.

Red and White Quinoa Salad
with Cucumber and Fresh Herbs

Chef Felipe Armenta grew up in Houston and got an early start in the business helping his family run restaurants there and later in San Angelo, where they still have Armenta's Café, Cork & Pig Tavern, and The Grill. When Felipe opened The Tavern in Fort Worth, I was taken with its unassumingly cozy atmosphere—including his cookbook collection, there for the browsing—and the spectacular attention paid to fresh vegetables. His newer restaurant, Pacific Table, keeps the vegetarian options interesting with a spicy pecan veggie burger and this winning quinoa salad. I love his recipe as written, though I sometimes substitute dried cranberries for half of the raisins. And, if you don't have all of the fresh herbs on hand, three out of the four will do just fine. This makes a flavorful side dish or a great light lunch.

4 to 6 servings (about 6 cups salad) : : **V** • **GF**

Salad

⅔ cup dried red quinoa

⅔ cup dried white or golden quinoa

Pinch of kosher salt

1 cup mixed raisins, chopped

½ large hothouse cucumber (about 6 ounces), chopped into ½-inch pieces (about 1 cup)

½ cup thinly sliced green onions (from about 8 green onions; use the white and pale green parts)

½ cup loosely packed fresh mint leaves, chopped

½ cup loosely packed fresh basil leaves, chopped

¼ cup loosely packed fresh tarragon leaves, chopped

¼ cup loosely packed fresh flat-leaf parsley leaves, minced

Vinaigrette

2 tablespoons cider vinegar

1 tablespoon plus 1 teaspoon organic granulated sugar

1 tablespoon Dijon mustard

2 teaspoons minced shallot (from about ¼ large shallot)

1 medium-size to large garlic clove, peeled and smashed

½ teaspoon (scant) kosher salt

½ teaspoon (scant) freshly ground black pepper

½ cup extra-virgin olive oil

Chopped Marcona almonds for garnish (optional)

RECIPE CONTINUES

To make the salad: Combine the red and white quinoa in medium, heavy saucepan or rice cooker.

Stir in 2⅔ cups of water and a pinch of salt. If using a rice cooker, cover the quinoa and turn on the rice cooker (it will shut off when the quinoa is done).

If using the stovetop method, cover the saucepan and bring the quinoa to a boil, then lower the heat to low and simmer, covered, until the quinoa is tender and the water has been absorbed (quinoa is done when a small white circle shows around each grain), 20 to 22 minutes.

Fluff the quinoa, then measure 4 cups of the cooked quinoa into a large bowl. Allow the quinoa to cool.

Add the raisins, cucumber, green onions, and all the herbs to the quinoa and toss to combine.

To make the vinaigrette: Combine the vinegar, sugar, mustard, shallot, garlic, salt, and pepper in a food processor or blender and purée. Add the olive oil in a slow stream to emulsify.

Drizzle the quinoa salad with the vinaigrette and toss to coat. Garnish the salad with the chopped almonds, if desired, and serve.

Nut-Crusted Goat Cheese Rounds

Add one of these rounds to each serving of your favorite green salad to make it main course-worthy. They can be fried or baked, although I've found that frying is a little more foolproof for yielding a crunchier, darker crust without overheating the cheese, keeping it creamy rather than grainy. Any soft, fresh goat cheese will work. In North Texas, some of the most interesting menus feature Latte Da Dairy's goat cheese, made in Flower Mound.

Makes about 4 rounds :: **Gluten-Free Option**

¾ cup raw pecan or walnut halves

1 large egg

⅓ cup unbleached all-purpose flour or almond meal (for gluten-free, if desired)

4 ounces soft, fresh goat cheese

Olive or canola oil for frying or baking

RECIPE CONTINUES

Coarsely grind the raw nuts in a food processor, or finely chop them on a cutting board; transfer to a shallow bowl.

In another shallow bowl, whisk the egg and 1 tablespoon of water to blend. Place the flour or almond meal in a third shallow bowl.

Slice the goat cheese into four equal pieces. Gently press each into a ½-inch-thick round, pressing around the edges to compact the cheese into shape. Dip all four rounds into the flour or almond meal, turning each to completely coat.

Next, dip all four rounds into the egg mixture, turning each to coat completely and allowing any excess egg to drip back into the bowl.

Finally, dip all four rounds into the ground nuts, turning to coat and gently pressing the nuts into the cheese to adhere. Place the nut-crusted goat cheese rounds on small plate; cover and refrigerate until just before serving time. Can be prepared up to a day ahead of time. Keep chilled.

If you want to fry them, pour enough oil into a small, heavy skillet to reach a depth of ¼ inch. Heat the oil over medium-high heat. Line a small plate with a paper towel. When the oil is hot enough to sizzle when you drop a nut in, add the goat cheese rounds and fry, turning once, until the crust is dark golden brown and crisp, about 2 minutes total.

Using a slotted spoon, transfer the goat cheese rounds to the paper towel-lined plate.

If you want to bake the rounds: Preheat the oven to 450°F. Line a small baking dish with parchment paper.

Using a pastry brush, lightly brush each goat cheese round all over with the oil. Place in the prepared dish and bake until the nut crust is light golden brown and the cheese is soft, 8 to 10 minutes. Serve the warm goat cheese atop individual servings of salad.

WINE: The zippy acidity of Sauvignon Blanc would definitely pair with the tangy goat cheese, but the pecans require something broader. Try an Albariño, such as from Spicewood Vineyards, when serving these patties with green salad. This Spanish varietal still brings the acidity, but with a little more mouthfeel and concentration.

Savory Zucchini Soup with Basil and Lemon Zest

This recipe comes from chef Molly McCook of Ellerbe Fine Foods in Fort Worth, a casually elegant restaurant in an old filling station on Magnolia Avenue. Ellerbe has gotten consistently positive reviews since opening in 2009; Molly has since cooked at the James Beard House in New York. The chef is a former vegetarian herself and the restaurant's menu attests to her heightened interest in local farm-to-market produce. Even in the Texas heat, it's relatively easy to grow zucchini and other summer squash. Molly offers this fantastic summer soup—served warm or chilled—for using a bumper crop of zucchini or yellow summer squash, or a combination of the two. Although she uses an artful thyme bouquet to infuse the soup with the herb's flavor, in my home kitchen, I never use cooking twine (there are so few things to truss when you're vegetarian), so I just throw in some thyme leaves. Note that Parmesan cheese is an optional garnish; the soup may be prepared vegan if you leave that off (and use vegan stock), and it's fantastic either way.

RECIPE CONTINUES

⅓ cup extra-virgin olive oil

1 large onion, diced

½ bunch thyme sprigs, tied with a string, or
   1 teaspoon fresh thyme leaves

2½ to 2¾ pounds fresh zucchini or yellow
   summer squash or a combination of the two
   (about 7 medium-size), trimmed, cut into
   ¾-inch-thick rounds

1 cup loosely packed fresh basil leaves,
   chopped

1 cup loosely packed fresh flat-leaf parsley
   leaves, chopped

2 garlic cloves, peeled and minced

1½ to 2 teaspoons kosher salt

Pinch of freshly ground black pepper

4 cups low-sodium vegetable stock (vegan, if
   desired)

Zest of 1 lemon for garnish

Extra-virgin olive oil for garnish

Grated Parmesan cheese for garnish (optional;
   omit for vegan)

Heat the olive oil in a medium, heavy pot over medium heat.

Add the onion and thyme bouquet and sauté until the onion is translucent, about 5 minutes.

Add the zucchini, basil, parsley, garlic, 1½ teaspoons of salt, and the pepper. Continue to sauté over medium heat for 5 minutes longer.

Add the stock, cover, and bring to a boil. Lower the heat to low and simmer until the zucchini is very tender and begins to break down, 20 to 25 minutes. Remove from the heat and discard the thyme bouquet.

Using a handheld immersion blender, purée the soup in the pot until it is completely smooth and creamy in texture, with small green flecks remaining. (Alternatively, working in batches, use a standing blender, filling it no more than half full, to purée the soup, returning it to the pot before continuing.) Season to taste with additional salt and pepper, if desired.

Ladle the soup into shallow bowls—it can be served warm or chilled. Garnish it with the lemon zest, drizzle it with the olive oil, and sprinkle it with the Parmesan, if desired.

Spicy Tortilla Soup

Tortilla soup is traditionally made with chicken, or at the very least chicken broth, which means most restaurant versions are off-limits to the meatless. This version of the steaming soup topped with crunchy tortilla strips and creamy avocado is suitable for just about everyone. Include as many of the suggested toppings as possible; they aren't merely garnishes—with tortilla soup, they *make* the dish. Homemade corn tortillas (page 173), which are a little thicker than store-bought ones, are especially good in this; it's a great way to use up day-old ones.

Makes about 6 servings (7 to 8 cups) : : **Vegan Option • GF**

Crispy Tortilla Strips

2 tablespoons canola or olive oil

6 corn tortillas (vegan and/or gluten-free, if desired)

Pinch of kosher salt

Soup

2 tablespoons canola or olive oil

1 large white or yellow onion, coarsely chopped

1 large poblano chile, stemmed, seeded, and coarsely chopped

4 large or 6 small garlic cloves, peeled and minced

1 teaspoon chili powder

1 teaspoon ground cumin

½ teaspoon garlic powder (gluten-free, if desired)

6 cups vegetable stock, or 6 cups water plus 2 cubes vegetable bouillon (vegan, if desired)

1 (14.5-ounce) can fire-roasted crushed or diced tomatoes with green chiles

½ to ¾ of a chipotle chile in adobo sauce (from a 7-ounce can; gluten-free, if desired)

Diced fresh avocado, for serving

Finely chopped red onion, for serving

Fresh cilantro leaves, for serving

Lime wedges, for serving

Shredded Cheddar or Monterey Jack cheese, for serving (optional; omit for vegan)

Sour cream, for serving (optional; omit for vegan)

Salt (optional)

RECIPE CONTINUES

To make the crispy tortilla strips: Line a large plate with a paper towel. Set aside.

Heat the oil in a medium, heavy nonstick skillet over medium-high heat. When the oil is hot, add one corn tortilla at a time, frying until puffed, crisp around edges, and beginning to brown in spots, turning once, 1 to 1½ minutes total.

Using tongs, transfer the cooked tortilla to the paper towel–lined plate to drain. Repeat with the remaining tortillas. Transfer the tortillas to a cutting board. Slice into ½-inch-wide strips, then slice the strips in half crosswise. Transfer the tortilla strips to a medium bowl, sprinkle with the salt, and toss to combine.

To make the soup: Heat the oil in a large, heavy soup pot over medium-high heat.

Add the onion and sauté until just beginning to turn translucent and soft, about 4 minutes. Add the poblano and sauté for 3 minutes longer. Add the garlic and sauté for 2 minutes longer.

Stir in the chili powder, cumin, and garlic powder. Stir in the stock, tomatoes, and chipotle chile. Cover the soup and bring to a boil. Lower the heat to medium-low and simmer, covered, until the onions and peppers are very tender and the flavors blend, about 35 minutes.

Using a handheld immersion blender, purée the soup. (Alternatively, working in batches, use a standing blender, filling it no more than half full, to purée the soup, returning it to the pot before continuing.) Season the soup to taste with salt, if desired.

Can be prepared up to 1 day ahead. Let cool, then cover and refrigerate. Bring to a simmer before continuing.

Ladle the hot soup into bowls. Top each with corn tortilla strips (they will soften as they sit in the soup). Serve, passing the additional toppings separately.

WINE: Loaded with spice and earth and red fruit flavors, Llano Estacado Reserve Tempranillo matches this soup practically note for note for complexity and excitement.

COCKTAIL: The Maurice-a-rita (page 218) was created for dishes like this.

BEER: Don't think light Mexican beer. Think hops. In fact, think *lots* of hops. A double IPA, such as the Brewer's Cut from Real Ale Brewing Company, meets the warm spice of the soup with cool caramel malt and crisp carbonation.

MAIN COURSES

I've noticed that oftentimes omnivores only *think* that they prefer meat; watch them closely, and you'll see. The first time I noticed it was on staff at *Bon Appétit* magazine, in the company of some of the most talented culinary minds I've ever known. When we'd work late, the staff would be treated to carryout at the office. But when faced with a large assortment of sandwiches, would the omnivores take a ham-and-cheese or chicken salad? No, they would not: They would choose the baguettes stuffed with grilled eggplant and goat cheese, or roasted portobello mushrooms and artichoke hearts. Anthony and I couldn't blame them—but we quickly learned that if we wanted dinner, we would need to beat them to the conference room. I've seen the pattern repeated often: When the meatless offerings are prepared with as much care as the meat, all bets are off. Consider Garlicky Pinto Bean and Brown Rice Burritos; Ratatouille with Creamy Polenta; Noodles with Fried Tofu and Spicy Peanut Sauce, Snow Peas, and Peppers; or Old-Fashioned Vegetable Pot Pie.

Garlicky Pinto Bean and Brown Rice Burritos

This is both a weeknight and casual party favorite around the Meyn house; everyone assembles their own, so there are never any complaints about what is or isn't in anyone's burrito. That said, for camping, picnicking, or even tailgating, these are easily assembled ahead of time and wrapped up in parchment and then foil. Canned beans will work in a pinch (preparing beans from scratch is very easy but does take some planning ahead). For a party, I like to go all out with freshly prepared beans, homemade salsa, and from-scratch guacamole—it really elevates the meal. The small fresh tortillas from Central Market—they come in such varieties as spelt, whole wheat, and, in late summer, Hatch—are our favorites for burritos.

Serves about 8 :: **Vegan Option**

16 small or 8 large flour, whole wheat, or spelt tortillas

2 cups brown rice, steamed according to the package instructions

Garlicky Pinto Beans (page 76)

Salsa (such as Fresh Tomato, Corn, and Pepper Salsa, page 22)

Guacamole (such as Guacamole with Tomato and Cilantro, page 20) or sliced fresh avocado

Shredded crisp lettuce, such as romaine

Sour cream for garnish (optional; omit for vegan)

Shredded Monterey Jack cheese for garnish (optional; omit for vegan)

Heat the tortillas over the open flame of a gas burner or on a nonstick pan or griddle, turning once, until warmed through and just beginning to puff. Serve the warm tortillas with the remaining ingredients.

WINE: A Syrah with a little age on it brings a seductive smokiness with it. Avoid young wines and look for Syrahs from the mid-2000s from Texas Hills Vineyard; they're rich with dark fruit flavors, warm spices, and hints of barbecue smoke.

BEER: Blonde ales crafted to be biscuity *and* spicy are the perfect beers for these burritos. My first choice would be Texas Backyard Blonde Ale from Fort Bend Brewing because the German malts and hops deliver that very appealing combination.

COCKTAIL: Try matching the Tex-Mex flavors of this dish with the Tex-Mex flavors of My Michelada (page 220).

Garlicky Pinto Beans

While canned beans are a well-loved convenience item that have earned their place in many a pantry, preparing beans from scratch is worth the effort when you have the time. In this version, a generous number of whole garlic cloves simmer until they're tender, almost melting into the beans.

Makes about 8 cups beans :: **V • GF**

1 pound dried pinto beans, rinsed

2 tablespoons kosher salt, for soaking beans, plus more to taste

1 large head of garlic, cloves separated and peeled

1 to 1½ teaspoons chipotle chili powder

Place the pinto beans in a colander and rinse well, picking out any that are shriveled or otherwise unappetizing. Place the beans in a large pot. Add 10 cups of water and the salt, stir, and soak for at least 8 hours and up to 24 hours.

Pour the beans into a colander to drain; rinse them well. Return the beans to the pot and add 7 cups of water and the garlic cloves. Cover and bring to a boil over medium-high heat. Lower the heat to low, cover, and simmer until the beans are tender, about 45 minutes longer (cooking time will vary depending on soaking time and freshness of the beans).

Season the beans to taste with additional kosher salt (I use about 1½ teaspoons) and chipotle chili powder. Serve warm.

BEANS FROM SCRATCH

There's nothing like dried beans to divide cooks into camps. You either soak them before cooking, claiming easier digestion and shorter cooking times, or you don't because you're convinced it's unnecessary and maybe even amateurish. You salt them from the beginning, or you wait until the very end, believing early salting will toughen the skins. You only trust your pressure cooker—or your slow cooker. All the conflicting opinions can make cooking beans from scratch seem like pretty complicated voodoo, when in fact, it's one of the easiest, thriftiest, and most satisfying kitchen tasks for preparing meatless meals.

From-scratch beans are far more appealing in taste and texture than canned, and are so healthful and versatile: Use them as a side dish, on crostini, or in burritos, salads, soups, and dips. While I'm a fan of soaking beans in brine before cooking, no matter how you soak, the most important thing for texture is that they're simmered gently, not rapidly, until they are very tender. Don't let a rogue bean convince you that the whole pot is perfectly cooked; taste at least four or five before taking them off the heat. Leftover beans freeze well; simply include some of the cooking liquid and seal in an airtight container.

Pinto Bean Chili or Meatless in Cowtown Frito Pie

When we moved to Texas and my husband joined the faculty of Texas Christian University, we accepted the serious responsibility that came with it to follow college football. TCU's Horned Frogs are the pride of Fort Worth, and it was for one of their away games that I hosted my first-ever "football-watching party," a task that, not having ever been a sports fan, seemed somewhat exotic. We bought plenty of Texas beer, and I began preparing a giant pot of vegetarian chili, a recipe I've made every fall for years. But the Texas crowd coming inspired me to buy a bag of Fritos to serve with it, and that was the tipping point: The compliments rolled in as they happily loaded up their bowls with chili, grated Cheddar, fresh cilantro, sour cream, red onions, and, of course, Fritos. And that is how you make a Meatless in Cowtown Frito Pie. (Fritos happen to be vegan and gluten free—and so is this recipe if you choose your toppings accordingly.)

Makes 14 to 16 servings :: **Vegan Option • GF**

2 pounds dried pinto beans

2 tablespoons kosher salt, for soaking beans

¼ cup olive oil

2 medium-size yellow onions, finely chopped

6 garlic cloves, peeled and minced

¼ cup chili powder

½ teaspoon chipotle chili powder or cayenne pepper

1½ teaspoons ground cumin

1 (6-ounce) can tomato paste

7 cups vegetable stock, or 7 cups water plus 2 cubes vegetable bouillon (vegan, if desired)

1 (16-ounce) bag frozen white corn kernels

1 (15-ounce) can tomato sauce

1 cup loosely packed fresh cilantro leaves, chopped

Grated sharp cheddar cheese for garnish (optional; omit for vegan)

Finely chopped red onion for garnish (optional)

Sour cream for garnish (optional; omit for vegan)

Fritos for garnish (optional)

RECIPE CONTINUES

Place the pinto beans in a colander and rinse them well, picking out any that are shriveled or otherwise unappetizing. Place the beans in a large, heavy soup pot, and add enough water to cover the beans by 3 inches. Stir in the kosher salt, and soak the beans for at least 8 hours and up to 24 hours.

After soaking, pour the beans into a colander to drain, rinse well, then return the beans to the pot. Add enough water to cover the beans by 2 to 3 inches. Bring to a boil over medium-high heat, then lower the heat to low, cover, and simmer until the beans are almost tender, about 45 minutes longer (cooking time will vary depending on the soaking time and freshness of the beans). Drain the beans in a colander and set aside.

Heat the olive oil in the large, heavy soup pot over medium heat. Add the onions and sauté until fragrant and tender, 10 to 15 minutes. Add the garlic and stir 1 minute. Stir in the chili powders and cumin, then the tomato paste. Add the stock, corn, and tomato sauce.

Stir in the prepared beans. Cover and bring to a boil, then lower the heat to medium-low and simmer until the beans are tender and the flavors meld, about 45 minutes.

Stir in a handful of chopped fresh cilantro, and serve with the remaining cilantro and additional toppings, such as grated cheese, red onion, sour cream, and Fritos, if desired.

WINE: While several full-bodied white wines would pick up on the veggie vibrancy of this chili, the addition of Fritos means something more substantial is fitting. Don't go overboard with a heavy Cabernet Sauvignon; instead a medium-bodied Syrah would hit the mark here. Try the Kiepersol Estates Syrah, which leans to the leaner side of the varietal yet still has a creamy—but not cloying—finish.

BEER: To complement the chili's earthy flavors, brown ale would be a fantastic choice. Real Ale's Brewhouse Brown Ale delivers dry chocolate and coffee flavors, with enough nut and malt notes to remain lively throughout.

Black Bean and Quinoa Chili

This recipe comes from Anthony's wife, Michele; we're certain that some Texan is reading this and shouting, "Real chili doesn't have beans!" Point taken (see page 82). But whatever you want to call this, don't be intimidated by quinoa. This incredibly nutritious grain provides hearty consistency and a slightly nutty flavor that marries deliciously with black beans. To dress up this thick chili, serve it with an array of toppings, such as green onion, cilantro, and sliced avocado, and crumbled cotija or shredded Cheddar cheese.

Makes 10 to 12 servings :: **Vegan Option • GF**

2 tablespoons olive oil

1 small or ½ medium-size yellow onion, diced

1 green bell pepper, stemmed, seeded, and chopped

1 poblano chile, stemmed, seeded, and finely diced

3 garlic cloves, peeled and minced

3 tablespoons chili powder

1 teaspoon ground cumin

1 teaspoon onion powder

3 cups vegetable stock (vegan, if desired)

3 (15-ounce) cans black beans, drained

1 (15-ounce) can diced tomatoes (do not drain) or 1 (10-ounce) can Ro*Tel diced tomatoes and green chiles (for a spicier version)

2 cups frozen or fresh corn kernels, or 1 (15.5-ounce) can white hominy, drained and rinsed

1 cup dried white or golden quinoa

1 cinnamon stick

½ teaspoon salt

½ teaspoon freshly ground black pepper

⅓ cup fresh cilantro leaves, chopped, plus more for garnish

Thinly sliced green onion for garnish (optional)

Sliced avocado for garnish (optional)

Crumbled cotija or shredded Cheddar cheese for garnish (optional; omit for vegan)

RECIPE CONTINUES ▶

Heat the oil in a large, heavy pot over medium-high heat. Add the onion and sauté until tender and translucent, about 3 minutes. Add the bell pepper and chile and sauté until just beginning to soften, about 3 minutes longer. Add the garlic and stir until fragrant, about 2 minutes longer. Stir in the chili powder, cumin, and onion powder.

Stir in the stock, 2 cups of water, and the black beans, tomatoes, corn, quinoa, cinnamon stick, salt, and pepper. Cover and bring to a rolling boil. Lower the heat to medium-low and simmer, covered, until the quinoa is tender and the flavors meld, about 40 minutes. Using tongs, remove the cinnamon stick and discard it. Stir in the cilantro and serve warm with additional cilantro and green onion, and avocado and cheese, if desired.

BEANS IN THE CHILI

If you ask native Texans about chili, they will tell you (politely, at first) that it's only "chili" if it's all-meat and no beans. In order to not just be bean soup, some vegetarian chili recipes try to follow the logic of this tradition by using textured vegetable protein (also known as TVP, rather unfortunately) to mimic meat's taste and texture. There are other ways of "beefing" up the chili (see a quinoa version on page 81), but of course, this still leaves the issue of having beans. In fact, if you ask vegeTexans, like us, about *real* Texas chili, we'll tell you (politely, at first) that it's only "chili" if its all-beans and no meat.

Enchiladas for a Crowd

Every summer, four generations of my family gather at an ancestral home on the Gulf coast for vacation. We take turns with meal-planning and cooking for the crowd, and my sister Katherine Brown and I always collaborate on a Mexican-style dinner. We perfected this rich enchilada recipe together. It serves about twelve, as long as you have some sides, too. Pass bowls of brown rice, black beans, shredded lettuce, salsa, sour cream, and guacamole on the side. At home, I'll make this recipe when a friend or neighbor needs a hot meal—it makes two pans of enchiladas, so there's one to drop off and one to keep. If you use freshly steamed Homemade Corn Tortillas (page 173) instead of store-bought: you can skip the step of warming them in oil, as they'll already be soft enough to roll.

Serves 10 to 12 :: **GF**

2 (15-ounce) cans tomato sauce

2 tablespoons chili powder

4 garlic cloves, peeled and minced

1 teaspoon ground cumin

24 ounces Monterey Jack cheese, grated

1 medium-size sweet onion, finely chopped

1 cup (8 ounces) sour cream, plus more for serving

½ cup loosely packed fresh cilantro leaves, coarsely chopped

Canola oil

24 corn tortillas (gluten-free, if desired)

Combine the tomato sauce, 1⅓ cups of water, and the chili powder, garlic cloves, and cumin in a large, heavy saucepan. Bring to a boil, stirring occasionally, then lower the heat to medium-low and simmer, uncovered, until slightly thickened, about 5 minutes. Remove from the heat and set aside.

Set aside 2 cups of the grated cheese to top the enchiladas later. In a large bowl, combine the remaining grated cheese, chopped onion, sour cream, and cilantro. Use a rubber spatula to mix it up well.

Line a large plate with paper towels. Pour enough oil into a heavy nonstick skillet to coat it; heat it over medium heat. Add as many tortillas as will fit in a single layer and cook, turning once, until the tortillas soften and begin to puff, 1 to

2 minutes, adding more oil as necessary for subsequent batches. Transfer the tortillas to the paper towel–lined plate to drain and repeat until all of the tortillas are cooked.

Preheat the oven to 375°F.

Using a scant ¼ cup of cheese filling for each, fill each tortilla, roll it up, and place it seam-side down in 13 x 9 x 2-inch baking dish, fitting twelve filled tortillas into each of two baking dishes.

Pour half of the sauce over each dish of enchiladas, drizzling evenly so all of the enchiladas are covered with sauce. Sprinkle 1 cup of the reserved cheese over each casserole.

Cover each casserole dish with foil and bake for 20 minutes. Uncover and bake until the sauce bubbles and the enchiladas are baked through, about 12 minutes longer. Serve warm.

RECIPE CONTINUES ►

WINE: Messina Hof Beau (Shiraz, Cabernet Franc, Muscat, Muscat Canelli) brings the touch of sweetness that pairs so well with spicy foods. Don't make the mistake of drinking a heavy red here: Medium-bodied varietals—or a cuvée of varietals—respond better to Mexican and Tex-Mex dishes.

BEER: A beer that features dark, robust flavors without being too dark and too robust is perfect for enchiladas. Spoetzl Brewing Company's Shiner Bock offers just the right amount of dark malty character delivered in a refreshing amber lager style.

DON'T ASK, DON'T TELL

When I was younger, I was more militant in my vegetarianism. Not that I ever pushed it on anybody, but stricter in the sense that I was ever-vigilant about never letting a spoonful of vegetable soup or a forkful of refried beans or a handful of French fries past my lips without ensuring there was no meat, fish, or fowl in them, including the cooking mediums.

Times change and so do people. Some people, at least. My wife, Michele, and I have both been vegetarians for many years—but we both also love a heaping, hot (be careful, it's *really* hot) platter of cheese enchiladas with rice and beans pretty much any time of the day or night, no matter where we are. Our favorite local Mexican restaurants (we've assured ourselves) use no lard in the tortillas or beans, and no chicken broth elsewhere. But when we're on the road, we've adopted a Don't Ask, Don't Tell policy when ordering at Mexican restaurants that covers the rice, beans, and tortillas. We enjoy our meal but never ask the waiter about those items, nor do we dwell on them during our meal. (I do wish Michele would realize that musing aloud about the meal's components in the car afterward is verboten, too.) A lot of Mexican restaurants here don't use lard in their cooking at all. There have been some that we've certainly had our suspicions about, but we knew the risks we were taking when we walked into the joint in the first place.

Am I a heretic and a traitor to the vegetarian nation? I don't think so, although some might disagree. But to paraphrase the words of my esteemed co-author, "I'm not ready to fight over a plate of Mexican food." —Anthony

Noodles with Fried Tofu and Spicy Peanut Sauce, Snow Peas, and Peppers

This colorful meal is fragrant, comforting, and vegan; it's also gluten-free if you use gluten-free noodles. Pressing the tofu before cooking helps to rid it of excess water, making for a more compact, pleasing texture, but if you're in a hurry that's a step you can skip. Making the sauce in a blender means natural peanut butter works just fine, as it whirs into a smooth, creamy sauce—no need to use the more highly processed, sweetened peanut butter. Because my household includes intermittently picky eaters (children's taste buds can be a moving target), I serve the vegetables on a separate platter, and the noodles and tofu tossed together with the peanut sauce. On my plate, I like it all together.

Makes about 6 servings :: **V • Gluten-Free Option**

Spicy Peanut Sauce

¼ cup coarsely chopped peeled fresh ginger (from about a 3-inch piece)

2 garlic cloves, peeled and coarsely chopped

½ cup natural peanut butter (I use salted but unsweetened)

¼ cup freshly squeezed lime juice (from 2 to 3 limes)

¼ cup tamari

1 tablespoon organic light or dark brown sugar

1 tablespoon sriracha, plus more to taste

Tofu and Noodles

1 (12-ounce) package extra-firm tofu

1 (12-ounce) package soba (Japanese buckwheat noodles) or 1 to 2 (8-ounce) packages rice noodles (gluten-free, if desired)

2 tablespoons olive oil

Vegetables

2 tablespoons olive oil

½ large yellow onion, sliced into rings about ⅓-inch thick, then sliced in half (about 1 generous cup)

1 medium-size red bell pepper, seeded and sliced lengthwise into ⅓-inch-thick strips (about 1 generous cup)

1 medium-size yellow bell pepper, seeded and sliced lengthwise into ⅓-inch-thick strips (about 1 generous cup)

6 ounces fresh snow peas, sliced in half on diagonal

Tamari or soy sauce (to taste; use tamari for gluten-free)

To make the sauce: Using a blender, mince the ginger and garlic. Add the peanut butter, ½ cup of water, and the lime juice, tamari, brown sugar, and sriracha and blend until the sauce is smooth. Season to taste with additional sriracha, if desired.

To make the tofu and noodles: Line a large dinner plate or a cutting board with a clean dish towel. Drain the tofu, rinse it, pat it dry, and place it on the towel-lined surface. Wrap the ends of the dish towel over the tofu to cover it completely. Top it with a second dinner plate or cutting board, and add two or three cans (or similar weight) to press the tofu. Let it stand for at least 45 minutes and up to 2 hours.

Slice the pressed tofu horizontally into eight slabs, then cut each slab in half to make sixteen squares. (If you skipped pressing the tofu, then let the tofu drain on a kitchen towel.)

Prepare the noodles according to the package instructions. Pour the prepared noodles into a colander and drain well.

Line a plate with paper towels. Heat the oil in a large, nonstick skillet over medium-high heat. Add the tofu and cook until golden brown on both sides, turning once, about 10 minutes total. Transfer to the paper towel-lined plate to drain.

To make the vegetables: Heat the oil in very large, heavy skillet over medium-high heat. Add the onion and sauté until soft and translucent, about 5 minutes. Add the peppers and sauté until beginning to soften, about 3 minutes longer. Add the snow peas and sauté until bright green and crisp-tender, about 4 minutes longer.

Season the vegetables to taste with tamari or soy sauce, stirring well. Remove from the heat and transfer to a serving platter.

To serve: Return the noodles to the pot and add just enough peanut sauce to coat the noodles.

Toss the noodles and peanut sauce over medium-low heat until heated through and coated, about 2 minutes. Add the fried tofu to the noodles and sauce, tossing gently to coat. Transfer the noodles and tofu to a large serving platter or bowl. Transfer the remaining peanut sauce to a small pitcher.

Serve the vegetables and noodles, passing the remaining spicy peanut sauce separately.

WINE: Try the Lost Oak Winery's Riesling with this dish. There's just something about the stone fruit, honey, and mineral notes of a dry Riesling that pairs so well with the exotic flavors of Asia.

BEER: Belgian ales work really well with a broad swath of spicy Asian cuisine. Take Shiner White Wing for instance: It's a thirst-quencher, for sure. But it's also got that hint of sweetness to play counterpoint to the spicy and savory peanut sauce.

Pizza Margherita with Shiner Bock Crust

Whether we bake it in the oven or grill it outside, homemade pizza is an all-ages favorite. Pizza dough is easy to make, you just have to plan ahead. This dough is cold-proofed, which means the liquid added is room temperature instead of warm (no thermometer necessary) and that it develops in the fridge more slowly. It's great after a full twenty-four hours, and arguably even better after two or three days. Mix up a batch of dough on Thursday and you'll have an easy Friday, Saturday, or Sunday pizza night to look forward to. If you're cooking for two to four, use half of the pizza dough and save the rest for another night. Most pizza dough recipes use water, but a bottle of Texas's well-loved Shiner Bock gives it much more flavor. This recipe is for a basic pizza; see page 93 for more ideas. The dough and sauce are vegan, so feel free to experiment with dairy-free shredded cheese if that's your thing.

Makes about 8 servings

Crust

3 cups unbleached bread flour

1 cup white whole wheat flour

1 (¼-ounce) package (about 2¼ teaspoons) rapid-rise yeast

1 teaspoon kosher salt

1 (12-ounce) bottle Shiner Bock beer, at room temperature (Samuel Adams Black Lager or even Michelob AmberBock will do a in a pinch)

¼ cup extra-virgin olive oil, plus more for coating bowl

Cornmeal, for dusting pan

Assembly

Easy No-Cook San Marzano Tomato Sauce (page 92)

1 pound whole-milk mozzarella cheese, coarsely grated (4 to 5 cups), or 1 pound fresh mozzarella, very thinly sliced

4 ounces shredded Parmesan cheese (about 1 cup)

6 garlic cloves, peeled, smashed, minced

1 cup loosely packed fresh basil leaves, slivered

Extra-virgin olive oil

To make the crust: Combine both of the flours, yeast, and salt in a large bowl. Use an electric mixer fitted with a dough hook to mix the ingredients on low speed.

With the mixer still on low speed, slowly pour in the room-temperature beer and the oil, mixing until a dough ball forms, then turn off the mixer and knead the dough a little with your hands if necessary (the dough will be soft and a little sticky).

Oil a large mixing bowl with olive oil. Transfer the dough to the oiled bowl, cover with a kitchen towel, and let stand at room temperature for 1 hour. Remove the towel, cover with plastic wrap, and refrigerate for at least 24 hours and up to 3 days. When ready to prepare the pizza, remove the dough from the refrigerator and let it stand at room temperature for 2 hours.

To bake the pizza

Arrange an oven rack in the top third of the oven. Preheat the oven to 550°F. Line a baking sheet with parchment paper and sprinkle lightly with cornmeal (the cooking time is so brief that the parchment will be okay even at the high temperature).

Divide the dough into quarters. Flatten one quarter of the dough in your hands, rotating and flipping from hand to hand to further flatten it. Place a dough disk on the prepared parchment paper and use your fingertips to push it into a 10- to 11-inch circle.

Spread a light layer of sauce over the pizza. Top with one quarter of the mozzarella, Parmesan, and garlic. Bake until the crust is golden and the cheese is melted and bubbling, 6 to 7 minutes. (Begin preparing the next pizza on cornmeal-dusted parchment paper while the first pizza is cooking.)

Remove the pizza from the oven and sprinkle it with one quarter of the fresh basil. Let it stand for 5 minutes. Drizzle lightly with extra-virgin olive oil, if desired, before slicing and serving. Repeat with the remaining dough, sauce, and toppings. Serve warm.

To grill the pizza

Preheat the grill to medium-high heat (about 425°F). Line two baking sheets with parchment paper and sprinkle lightly with cornmeal. Divide the dough into eight equal portions to make individual-size pizzas that are easy to handle on the grill. Flatten one-eighth of the dough in your hands, rotating and flipping from hand to hand to further flatten it. Place a dough disk on the prepared parchment paper and use your fingertips to push it into a 6-inch circle. Repeat with the remaining dough, arranging four pizza crusts on each of the two baking sheets.

Place the prepared pizza sauce, each of the cheeses, garlic, basil, and additional olive oil into separate bowls; arrange the bowls on a tray. Take the dough, tray of ingredients, a pastry brush, and large spatula outside to the grill with you.

Brush each of the pizza crusts generously over the top with olive oil. Using the spatula, loosen each of four crusts from the tray and turn the crusts onto the preheated grill, oiled side down. Close the grill and cook until grill marks show and the crusts are baked through underneath, about 1½ minutes.

Open the grill and brush the tops of each crust with olive oil. Turn the crusts over to the second side. Working quickly, spread a light layer of sauce over each pizza crust. Top each with one-eighth of the mozzarella, Parmesan, and garlic. Close the grill and cook until the crusts are golden and the cheese is melted and bubbling, 2 to 3 minutes longer. Using the spatula, transfer the cooked pizzas back to the baking sheet and sprinkle each with one-eighth of the basil. Drizzle lightly with additional extra-virgin olive oil, if desired. Repeat with the remaining pizza crusts, oil, sauce, cheeses, garlic, and basil.

Let the pizzas stand for 5 minutes before slicing and serving.

WINE: This is a no-brainer, right? Sangiovese—the classic Italian varietal—is a perfect pizza pairing. Duchman Family Winery Sangiovese is brimming with earthy spices and acidity that pops when enjoyed with tomato-sauce dishes.

BEER: This is a no-brainer, too, right? You got Shiner Bock in the crust. So you drink Spoetzle Brewery's Shiner Bock. Or, you drink a pilsner, like Shiner 101 Czech-Style Pilsner, which has a full mouthfeel yet delicate herb and grass notes that pair nicely with the sauce.

Easy No-Cook San Marzano Tomato Sauce

Sure, you can buy a jar of pizza sauce, but if you buy a can of sweet, low-acidity San Marzano tomatoes instead, you'll have a quick sauce that's sublime and so simple. I also use this sauce in my Grilled Eggplant Parmesan with Fresh Basil (page 112).

Makes about 1¾ cups sauce :: **V • GF**

2 garlic cloves

1 (28-ounce) can whole San Marzano tomatoes (or other plum tomatoes), drained

1 tablespoon extra-virgin olive oil

½ teaspoon balsamic vinegar

Kosher salt

Red pepper flakes

Chop the garlic in a food processor.

Gently squeeze out some of the extra juice from the canned tomatoes (they don't need to be dry) before adding the tomatoes to the garlic in the food processor.

Add the olive oil and vinegar and blend to a purée. Season to taste with salt and red pepper flakes, blending again.

Can be prepared up to 2 days ahead of time. Cover and refrigerate.

THREE MORE PIZZAS

Pizza is great for casual gatherings; prepare the crusts, sauce, and a variety of toppings, and invite guests to customize their pies.

1. Pineapple, feta, jalapeño, and onion: Cut off the top and bottom of a fresh pineapple. Slice away the rough peel, and slice the pineapple off its core. Cut enough of the pineapple into small, bite-size chunks to top your pizza (save any extra pineapple for another use). Seed and mince one jalapeño pepper. Mince $1/2$ medium-size white onion. Top the unbaked pizza with sauce and mozzarella, then pineapple, feta, jalapeño, and onion. Bake the pizza.

2. Fresh spinach: Before adding the cheese, pile fresh baby spinach leaves high atop the sauce on the unbaked pizza (the spinach will shrink down in the oven), then sprinkle the pizza with mozzarella and Parmesan cheese and bake until the spinach wilts and the cheese melts, bubbles, and begins to brown in spots.

3. Mushroom and caramelized onion: Sauté $1/2$ large onion, thinly sliced, in 1 tablespoon of olive oil until tender and browned, about 8 minutes. Add $1/2$ teaspoon of balsamic vinegar; transfer the onion to a plate. Add another tablespoon of olive oil to the skillet and sauté 8 ounces of chopped cremini mushrooms until browned, 6 to 8 minutes. Deglaze the pan with $1/4$ cup Chardonnay, cooking until it's absorbed. Skip the pizza sauce, and top the pizza with mozzarella, Parmesan, caramelized onions, and mushrooms, and then bake.

Ratatouille with Creamy Polenta

This traditional stew of summer's best produce takes a little bit of thinking ahead—soaking the polenta, letting the eggplant sweat it out in a colander—but when it's time to start cooking, it all comes together easily enough. A summer garden in Texas, and in many other parts of the country, of course, can provide all the vegetables needed. Browning each vegetable separately ensures perfectly cooked ingredients as well as rich, hearty flavors.

Makes about 8 servings :: **Vegan Option • GF**

2 pounds eggplant (about 2 medium-size) cut into ¾-inch cubes

1¼ teaspoons kosher salt, divided, plus more to taste

½ cup olive oil, divided

2 pounds zucchini (about 4 medium-size), cut lengthwise in half and crosswise into ¾-inch pieces

1 pound green bell peppers (about 2 large), seeded and cut into ¾-inch pieces

1 large sweet onion, chopped (about 2 cups)

1 head of garlic, cloves separated, peeled, and coarsely chopped

1½ pounds tomatoes, seeded and chopped (2½ to 3 cups)

¼ cup loosely packed slivered fresh basil

Creamy Polenta (page 95)

Shredded Parmesan cheese, for serving (optional; omit for vegan)

Place the eggplant cubes in a colander and sprinkle with 1 teaspoon of the salt, tossing to coat. Let the eggplant drain 30 minutes. Pat the eggplant dry with a paper towel.

Heat 2 tablespoons of the olive oil in very large, heavy skillet over medium-high heat. Add the zucchini and sauté until beginning to brown in spots, 7 to 9 minutes. Transfer the zucchini to a large pot on the back burner (no heat).

Add 3 tablespoons of olive oil to the skillet and sauté the eggplant until beginning to brown in spots, 7 to 9 minutes. Add the eggplant to the zucchini.

Add 2 tablespoons of the olive oil to the skillet and sauté the green bell peppers until they are beginning to brown in spots, 7 to 9 minutes. Add the peppers to the other vegetables in the pot.

Add the remaining 1 tablespoon of olive oil to the skillet and sauté the onion and garlic until soft and fragrant, 5 to 7 minutes. Add to other vegetables. Remove the skillet from the heat.

Gently stir the tomatoes and 1 cup of water into the vegetables, cover, and bring to a simmer over medium-high heat. Lower the heat to low, cover, and let simmer, stirring occasionally, until the flavors meld and the vegetables are very tender, with the eggplant almost falling apart, 30 to 35 minutes.

Remove the ratatouille from the heat and stir in the basil and the remaining ¼ teaspoon of salt; season to taste with additional salt, if desired.

Fill shallow bowls with the warm Creamy Polenta, top it with ratatouille, and serve, passing the Parmesan separately, if desired.

Creamy Polenta

This simple dish makes a great base for the flavorful Ratatouille (page 94); it would also be wonderful topped with sautéed greens or mushrooms. Learning to soak Southern hominy grits before cooking them was an epiphany for me, and the method works just as well with corn grits, also known as polenta; the no-fuss technique produces creamy results. Look for local stone-ground cornmeal or polenta, such as that from Lamb's Grist Mill in Converse, Texas.

Makes about 8 servings : : **Vegan Option • GF**

6 cups vegetable stock, at room temperature (vegan, if desired)

1½ cups coarsely ground corn grits or polenta

½ cup half and half or (for vegan) Basic Cashew Cream (page 96)

½ cup grated Parmesan cheese (about 2 ounces) or (for vegan) 2 teaspoons nutritional yeast

Salt (optional)

Place the stock in a medium, heavy saucepan. Add the grits and whisk to blend well. Cover and let stand for at least 1 hour and up to 3 hours. Can be prepared 1 day ahead. Keep covered and refrigerate until ready to cook.

When you're ready to cook, rewhisk the mixture in the saucepan. Place the saucepan over medium-high heat, cover, and bring to a boil, whisking occasionally. Lower the heat to low, keeping the pot covered, and simmer until the polenta is thick and soft, whisking occasionally, about 10 minutes.

Remove from the heat. Whisk in the half-and-half or cashew cream and Parmesan or nutritional yeast. Season to taste with salt, if desired. Cover to keep warm until ready to serve.

WINE: Mourvèdre is a red grape from southern France that produces firm, tannic wines. Bending Branch Winery's Mourvèdre, however, is a softer version, with warm spice and jammy red and black fruit flavors that are wonderful with eggplant.

Basic Cashew Cream

I'll admit that I'm not a fan of products that rely on a long, strange ingredients list to approximate dairy, but it's hard to argue with the creamy deliciousness that results from soaked raw cashews blended with water. A blender is a must for this recipe; a food processor simply won't make it creamy enough. If you avoid dairy, try a bit of this homemade "cream" in place of its traditional counterpart in such dishes as the Creamy Polenta (page 95) and many others.

Makes 1 to 1¼ cups cashew cream :: **V • GF**

1 cup raw cashews

Place the cashews in a small bowl; add enough cold water to completely submerge them, cover, and refrigerate for at least 8 hours and up to overnight.

Drain the soaked cashews well, and transfer them to a standing blender. Add ½ cup plus 2 tablespoons of water and purée, scraping down the sides of the blender and blending again until the cashews are a very smooth, creamy consistency.

Transfer to a storage container, cover, and refrigerate until ready to use. Can be prepared up to 2 days ahead. Keep refrigerated.

Garlicky-Greens Spanakopita

Make this dish with any combination of your favorite frozen greens, such as spinach, kale, and chard. Be sure to begin thawing the phyllo and greens ahead of time. Although many recipes use melted butter to brush between the layers of pastry, olive oil also produces wonderful, flaky results—and it's a lot better for you. If you're not working quickly, you might find it necessary to cover your stack of phyllo with a slightly damp kitchen towel to keep it from drying out before you use it.

Serves 8 to 10 :: **Vegan Option**

¼ cup plus 2 tablespoons olive oil, or more as needed, divided

1 large yellow onion, chopped (about 2 cups)

1 bunch green onions, thinly sliced (8 to 9 whole; use white and pale green parts plus 1 inch of dark green for about 1 cup total)

6 garlic cloves, peeled and minced

1 (1-pound) bag frozen organic spinach, thawed in colander

1 (1-pound) bag frozen organic kale, thawed in colander

¼ cup pine nuts

1 tablespoon freshly squeezed lemon juice

½ teaspoon kosher salt

2 large eggs or (for vegan) flax eggs (page 141)

4 ounces feta cheese, crumbled (about 1 cup), or (for vegan) 1 (12-ounce) package extra-firm tofu, drained and coarsely crumbled

1 (1-pound) box organic phyllo dough sheets (you will need a little more than half the box), thawed in the refrigerator

RECIPE CONTINUES

Preheat the oven to 350°F. Heat 2 tablespoons of the olive oil in a large, heavy skillet over medium-high heat. Add the onion and sauté until soft and translucent, about 5 minutes. Add the green onions and sauté until soft, about 2 minutes. Add the garlic and sauté until fragrant and soft, about 2 minutes. Remove from the heat.

If frozen greens are not fully thawed, leave them in their colander and run warm water over them. Squeeze the liquid from the thawed greens, extracting as much moisture as possible. Place the greens, onion mixture, pine nuts, lemon juice, and salt in a food processor and pulse to coarsely chop.

Add the eggs or flax eggs and blend in until incorporated. Add the feta or tofu and pulse briefly to mix in, leaving some large bits of cheese or tofu. If using flax eggs and tofu, season to taste with additional salt, if desired.

Place a 13 x 9 x 2-inch casserole dish on a work surface. Pour the remaining ¼ cup of olive oil into a small bowl. Unfold the phyllo flat on your work surface. Working with two sheets at a time, drape the phyllo over the casserole dish, allowing the pastry to hang over the sides of the dish (meanwhile, cover the remaining phyllo from the package with a damp kitchen towel as needed).

Using a pastry brush, lightly brush the top layer of the phyllo with olive oil. Repeat with another two sheets of phyllo, brushing lightly all over with olive oil and repeating three more times for a total of five sets (ten sheets) of phyllo.

Transfer the greens mixture to the phyllo-lined dish, using a rubber spatula to spread it into an even thickness. Fold one sheet of remaining phyllo dough in half crosswise, placing the large rectangle atop the greens mixture to cover. Brush it lightly with olive oil. Repeat four more times. Trim some of the overhang from around the sides of the dish if you like less pastry; fold any remaining overhang over the top of the pie, brushing the top with olive oil.

Bake until the pastry is golden and the filling is puffed, 35 to 40 minutes. Let cool for 5 minutes. Cut into squares or rectangles and serve warm.

WINE: A zesty, citrusy Sauvignon Blanc, such as the one from Fall Creek Vineyards, would tingle the same taste buds as this pie—and might even ring a few new ones.

Grilled Pepper, Squash, and Mushroom Fajitas with Easy Tomatillo-Avocado Salsa Verde

An inexpensive perforated stainless-steel grill topper makes short work of grilling big batches of fajita filling (for more on the tool, see the sidebar on page 105). Cooking indoors? Try a large cast-iron skillet and sauté the vegetables over medium-high heat, working in batches to avoid crowding the pan. This recipe is vegan and can also be gluten-free if served with gluten-free tortillas. I like to serve these with rice and black beans on the side.

6 servings :: **V • Gluten-Free Option**

Marinade

¼ cup extra-virgin olive oil

2 tablespoons freshly squeezed lime juice (from about 1 lime)

½ teaspoon garlic powder

½ teaspoon ground cumin

½ teaspoon chili powder

¼ teaspoon kosher salt

Vegetables

8 ounces whole cremini mushrooms

1 large red bell pepper (6 to 8 ounces)

1 large orange bell pepper (6 to 8 ounces)

1 medium-size yellow squash (about 6 ounces), trimmed

1 medium-size zucchini squash (about 6 ounces), trimmed

1 medium-size yellow onion

Assembly

12 small flour or corn tortillas (gluten-free, if desired)

Easy Tomatillo-Avocado Salsa Verde (page 102)

RECIPE CONTINUES

To make the marinade: In a small bowl, whisk the olive oil, lime juice, garlic powder, cumin, chili powder, and salt to blend.

To make the vegetables: Gently wash the mushrooms and trim their stems; let them drain on a clean dish towel.

Halve both bell peppers and remove their seeds and stems; slice into ⅓- to ½-inch-thick slices. Transfer the pepper slices to a very large bowl. Slice the squash and zucchini diagonally into ⅓- to ½-inch-thick slices and add them to the peppers. Peel the onion and slice it into ⅓- to ½-inch-thick rings, separating the rings, and add to the other vegetables. Slice the mushrooms into ⅓- to ½-inch-thick slices and add to the other vegetables. Rewhisk the marinade and drizzle it over the vegetables; using your hands, toss to coat. Let the vegetables marinate while preparing the grill.

Place a perforated stainless-steel grill topper (see sidebar, page 105) directly on the grill grates. Heat the grill to medium-high heat (about 375°F).

Pour half of the vegetables onto the grill topper, watching for flare-ups from the oil. Using a long-handled metal spatula, spread the vegetables out in a single layer, close the grill, and grill until the vegetables are just beginning to brown on the underside, 4 to 5 minutes.

Using the spatula, carefully turn the vegetables over, close the grill, and continue grilling until just tender and beginning to brown on the second side, 4 to 5 minutes longer.

Transfer the vegetables to a serving platter and tent with foil to keep warm until ready to serve. Repeat with the second half of the vegetables, grilling on both sides and then transferring to the platter.

To assemble: Heat the tortillas directly over a gas flame or in a seasoned or nonstick skillet until heated through and just beginning to puff, turning once.

Serve the warm tortillas with the vegetables and the salsa verde for drizzling.

WINE: The sophisticated dark fruit flavors of Brennan Vineyards' Tempranillo pair nicely with the earthiness of this dish.

BEER: Finding a crisp American-style brown ale is key here. Real Ale's Brewhouse Brown has all the smoky dark flavors but with an engaging amount of carbonation to make it a great match for these fajitas.

Easy Tomatillo-Avocado Salsa Verde

Traditional salsa verde gets its green from generous helpings of tomatillos, chiles, and cilantro; avocado makes the perfect creamy addition. This easy salsa recipe is a delicious alternative to tomato-based renditions when you want something different with your fajitas—or chips, burritos, or tacos. While you can roast your own tomatillos for a from-scratch version, this one is delicious, and lots faster.

Makes about 1¼ cups salsa verde :: **V • GF**

1 cup prepared salsa verde (from a 12-ounce jar)

1 medium-size avocado, peeled and pitted

½ cup loosely packed fresh cilantro leaves

1 tablespoon freshly squeezed lime juice

In a food processor, combine the salsa verde, avocado, cilantro leaves, and lime juice. Blend until the mixture is coarsely puréed. Season to taste with salt.

Serve at room temperature or chilled. Can be prepared up to 2 days ahead. Cover and keep refrigerated.

FREEDOM FROM SKEWERS

For more years than I'd like to admit, grilling vegetables meant dutifully soaking bamboo skewers in water (so the skewers won't char), and then packing the skewers tightly with an array of colorful vegetables. Vegetables grilled this way do have a wonderful smoky flavor, but in my experience, the edges get charred while the middle is stuck on the "crisp" side of crisp-tender. But an inexpensive grill topper—an impulse buy that was less than $15—has changed the way I grill. It's just a perforated stainless-steel sheet with raised edges to keep the veggies from falling into the fire, and it makes short work of grilling big batches of fajita filling, Brussels sprouts, broccoli, and more. Not only is grilling this way far less time consuming than using skewers, it produces perfectly cooked vegetables—smoky but not charred.

Poblano Chiles Rellenos with Chipotle Sauce

Poblanos are sometimes mislabeled as "pasilla" chiles—simply look for dark green chiles that are slightly heart-shaped (fatter than Anaheim chiles but thinner than green bell peppers). I like to serve these with steamed brown rice (such as the Texas-grown Texmati) and a side of black beans (see page 118). Battering and frying is an effort, but it's worth it for this special-occasion dish. I buy chipotle chili powder in the bulk spice section at Central Market; if you can't find it, try any hot chili powder, using ¼ teaspoon at a time, and testing the heat before adding more (the sour cream cools things down a little, so prepare the sauce toward the top of your spicy threshold and you'll be happy with the results).

Makes 12 chiles (serves 6 to 12, depending on sides)

Chipotle Sauce

2 tablespoons olive oil

2 garlic cloves, peeled, crushed, and minced

2 tablespoons unbleached all-purpose flour

1 (15-ounce) can tomato sauce

1 teaspoon ground cumin

½ to 1 teaspoon chipotle chili powder

¼ cup sour cream

Poblano Chiles Rellenos

12 large poblano chiles

1 (10- to 12-ounce) wheel queso fresco

⅔ cup plus 6 tablespoons unbleached all-purpose flour, divided

6 large eggs

Light olive oil for frying

To make the sauce: Heat the olive oil in a small, heavy saucepan over medium heat.

Add the garlic and sauté until fragrant, about 2 minutes. Stir in the flour with a wooden spoon until the mixture is smooth and bubbling, about 2 minutes longer.

Whisk in the tomato sauce, 1 cup of water, and the cumin and chili powder (use the full teaspoon if you like heat), cover, and bring to a simmer, whisking occasionally. Remove from the heat and whisk in the sour cream. Cover to keep warm.

To make the chiles: Arrange an oven rack in the top third of the oven. Line a large baking sheet with two layers of overlapping foil (you'll need the extra foil to help steam the chiles after roasting). Spread out the chiles in single layer on the baking sheet. Roast the chiles under the broiler until the skins are blistered and browning, turning once with tongs and rotating the baking sheet for even roasting if necessary, 5 to 7 minutes per side.

Remove the baking sheet from the oven, gather the foil around the chiles, and pinch the ends of the foil together to seal; let the chiles steam until the skins pull off easily, about 15 minutes. Remove as much of the skin as possible. Seed the chiles by carefully cutting around the stem, taking care to keep the chiles intact, and removing the stem and as many of the seeds as possible (rinse them in water if needed to remove additional seeds, but do not slice the chiles open; any seeds left behind will simply add spiciness).

Cut the queso fresco into twelve equal wedges; crumble one wedge into each of the prepared chiles.

Place ⅔ cup of the flour in a shallow bowl.

Separate the eggs, placing the whites in a large mixing bowl and the yolks in medium mixing bowl. Using an electric mixer on high speed, beat the egg whites until stiff peaks form. Beat the egg yolks until thick and creamy. Using a rubber spatula, gently fold the yolks into the whites. Sprinkle the egg mixture with the remaining 6 tablespoons of flour and gently fold in.

Line a large plate or platter with paper towels. Pour the oil to a depth of 1 inch into a heavy skillet. Heat the oil between medium and medium-high heat. (It will take several minutes to heat up adequately; before frying, test a pea-size drop of batter—it should sizzle as soon as it hits the oil.)

When the oil is ready, dredge one stuffed chile into the flour in the shallow bowl, then into the egg batter, covering completely and taking care to keep the open end of the chile sealed by covering with the batter. Add the chile to the oil and fry, turning once, until the batter is golden brown, about 2 minutes total. Transfer the cooked chiles to the paper towel-lined plate to drain. Repeat with the remaining chiles, cooking batches of up to three or four at a time. Serve warm with the chipotle sauce. If not serving immediately, transfer the chiles to a baking dish and keep warm in the oven.

WINE: To stand up to the smoky chipotle sauce, Zinfandel is the way to go. Rabbit Ridge Winery Zinfandel is smooth and peppery and features a lingering finish of oak and vanilla.

BEER: Saint Arnold's Amber Ale pairs so well with this dish. It's crisp and refreshing with a medium body and slightly sweet mouthfeel.

COOKING WITH CHILES

Cooks in Texas make liberal use of chiles; not only are they loaded with flavor and heat, but also with vitamin C. It's important to remember that the heat is concentrated in the seeds and ribs, so if you're seeding one of the hotter varieties, put on rubber gloves. Since moving to Texas, I've learned the hard way that a fairly fierce burning sensation can last for several hours—even overnight—if you dig into seeding too many chiles with your bare fingers.

Charred and steamed chiles slip right out of their skins, ready to bring subtle, slow heat to a variety of dishes, whether used whole in rellenos or blended into hummus. While many recipes in this book include instructions for roasting chiles in the oven (see the Poblano Chiles Rellenos, page 103), the grill also is a great option. Preheat the grill to medium-high (about 425°F). Line a large platter with foil. Grill the chiles directly on the grill grates, closing the grill cover, until charred and blistering on the bottom, about 4 minutes. Use long tongs to turn the chiles over and roast them on the second side, about 4 minutes longer. Transfer the chiles to the foil-lined platter, fold the foil around them, pinching the edges to seal, and allow the chiles to steam for 15 minutes. Remove the chiles' skins and seeds, and use as directed in the recipe.

Mixed Mushroom Risotto with Parsley and Truffle Oil

The rice you choose will impact how much broth you need. Arborio will absorb somewhat less broth than Carnaroli. While it might be off-limits at most restaurants due to the dreaded, ubiquitous chicken broth, risotto is a natural at home for vegetarian, vegan, and gluten-free cooks. Serve this with a crisp green salad or sautéed greens.

Makes about 4 servings :: **Vegan Option • GF**

½ ounce mixed dried mushrooms, such as porcini, shiitake, and oyster

6 to 7 cups vegetable stock (vegan, if desired)

2 tablespoons olive oil

1 medium-size yellow onion, finely chopped (about 2 cups)

8 ounces fresh mushrooms, such as button, portobello, cremini, or a mix, chopped

3 garlic cloves, minced

1½ cups Carnaroli or Arborio rice

1 cup dry white wine

¼ cup heavy whipping cream or (for vegan) Basic Cashew Cream (page 96)

½ cup fresh flat-leaf parsley leaves, coarsely chopped

Kosher salt and freshly ground black pepper

About 2 teaspoons truffle oil

¼ cup lightly toasted pine nuts (optional)

½ cup grated Parmesan cheese (optional; omit for vegan)

RECIPE CONTINUES

Rinse the dried mushrooms well. Place in a small heatproof bowl and pour boiling water over the mushrooms to cover. Let stand for 15 minutes to soften. Drain, then transfer to a cutting board and mince.

Bring the stock to a gentle simmer in a medium, heavy pot.

Heat the olive oil in an extra-large, heavy skillet over medium-high heat. Add the onion and sauté until tender and translucent, 3 to 5 minutes.

Add the fresh and dried mushrooms and the garlic and sauté until the fresh mushrooms release their juices and begin to brown, about 5 minutes.

Add the rice and stir for 1 minute. Add the white wine and stir until the wine is absorbed. Add 1 cup of the hot stock and simmer, stirring frequently, until the stock is absorbed. Continue adding more hot stock, 1 cup at a time, stirring frequently, until the rice is cooked to the desired consistency (generally until it's just slightly al dente).

Stir in the cream or cashew cream and return to a simmer, stirring well. Stir in the chopped parsley. Adjust the seasoning to taste with salt and pepper. Spoon the risotto onto plates, and drizzle each portion with a few drops of truffle oil. Sprinkle with pine nuts and Parmesan cheese, if desired. Serve immediately.

WINE: Nebbiolo is an Italian red grape that offers delicious flavors of licorice, truffles, and wild cherry. Rancho Point Vineyard's Nebbiolo is a perfect accompaniment to this earthy risotto.

BEER: Jester King Brewery specializes in farmhouse ales, which are aged in oak barrels and provide tangy, sour notes. When enjoyed with Jester King's Boxer's Revenge the risotto might become your favorite weekday meal.

Falafel-Millet Patties
with Tahini-Cilantro Sauce

Traditional falafel gets even better with the addition of millet, a grain that's light and fluffy like couscous when it's cooked, but more healthful. I like these patties best when made small (plan on two to three per person), drizzled with the tahini sauce, and served alongside brown rice or quinoa and green beans. They can also be made into burger-size patties (use ½ cup of the mixture for each to make about seven large burgers) and served on a bun.

Makes about 6 servings :: **V • GF**

½ cup dried millet

3 tablespoon extra-virgin olive oil, or more as needed, divided

1 medium-size onion, chopped (about 2 cups)

3 garlic cloves, peeled, smashed, and coarsely chopped

½ cup garbanzo bean flour

1 teaspoon baking soda

½ teaspoon ground cumin

½ teaspoon ground coriander

½ teaspoon green chili powder, such as Anaheim (optional)

1 teaspoon kosher salt

1¾ cups Garlicky Garbanzo Beans (page 26) or 1 (15- to 15.5-ounce) can garbanzo beans, drained and rinsed

½ cup fresh cilantro leaves

2 tablespoons freshly squeezed lemon juice

Tahini-Cilantro Sauce (page 111)

RECIPE CONTINUES

Stir 1½ cups of water, the millet, and a pinch of salt together in a medium, heavy saucepan. Cover and bring to a boil. Lower the heat to low and simmer, covered, until the millet is fully cooked and all water is absorbed or evaporated, 20 to 22 minutes. Remove from the heat and fluff the millet with a fork (you will have about 2 cups of cooked millet).

In a large, heavy skillet, heat 1 tablespoon of the olive oil over medium-high heat. Add the onion and sauté until translucent and soft, about 5 minutes. Add the garlic and sauté for 1 minute longer. Remove from the heat.

In a medium bowl, whisk the garbanzo bean flour, baking soda, cumin, coriander, green chile powder, if using, and salt to blend.

In a food processor, combine the onion mixture with the beans, cilantro, and lemon juice, and pulse to chop. Add the garbanzo bean flour mixture and blend well (the mixture should be finely chopped but not completely puréed).

Add the millet, breaking it apart as you add it (it tends to clump after cooking), and pulse briefly, just long enough to combine.

The mixture can be prepared up to 1 day ahead of time. Cover and refrigerate until ready to cook.

Using ¼ cup of the mixture for each, form the dough into small patties, flattening with your hands (the dough will be soft).

Heat the remaining 2 tablespoons oil in a large, heavy nonstick skillet over medium-high heat. Cook half of the patties in the oil (do not crowd) until they are heated through and browned on both sides, carefully turning once, 4 to 5 minutes total (the patties will be very tender and will firm up as they cool). Repeat with additional oil, if necessary, and the remaining mixture. Serve warm with the Tahini-Cilantro Sauce.

Tahini-Cilantro Sauce

This vegan and gluten-free sauce makes a zippy alternative to sour cream-based sauces; it's also delicious drizzled over black beans and rice.

Makes about 1¼ cups sauce : : **V • GF**

½ cup tahini (sesame seed paste)

½ cup loosely packed fresh cilantro leaves

¼ cup freshly squeezed lime juice (from about 2 limes)

½ teaspoon garlic powder (gluten-free, if desired)

½ teaspoon kosher salt, or more to taste

Combine all the ingredients in a blender and blend until the cilantro is puréed. Season to taste with additional salt, if desired. Serve at room temperature or chilled. Can be prepared a day ahead. Cover and keep refrigerated.

WINE: Although Vermentino sounds like some rat-faced boss from *The Godfather*, it's actually a crisp, broad-flavored white wine. Duchman Winery produces one of the state's finest representations of this varietal.

BEER: An India Pale Ale (IPA) is a beer made especially hopped so it pairs with food. Community Beer Company's Mosaic IPA is a crisp, zesty beer that's perfect for falafel.

Grilled Eggplant Parmesan with Fresh Basil

Most restaurant versions of this classic dish include breaded and fried eggplant, and I made it that way at home for many years. Living in Texas, with its nearly year-round grilling weather, this fresh-tasting recipe with grilled eggplant now has more appeal. I like the eggplant thinly sliced, so I use a grill pan to avoid letting anything slip through the grates. If you grill it directly on the grates, it will brown faster, so watch it carefully. This saucy dish is wonderful served atop cooked spaghetti, or just with a simple green salad.

Makes 4 to 6 servings :: **GF**

2 large eggplants (about 1¾ pounds total)

About 1 teaspoon kosher salt, divided

1 recipe Easy No-Cook San Marzano Tomato Sauce (page 92)

About ¼ cup plus 2 tablespoons extra-virgin olive oil

½ pound fresh whole-milk mozzarella cheese, grated or thinly sliced and torn into coarse shreds

½ cup (about 2 ounces) freshly grated Parmesan cheese

¼ cup loosely packed fresh basil leaves, slivered

Cut the stems off the eggplants. Slice the eggplants lengthwise into ¼-inch-thick slices. Arrange the eggplant slices in single layer on a clean dish towel. Sprinkle the slices with kosher salt, using about ½ teaspoon. Let stand for 20 minutes.

Using another clean dish towel or paper towel, blot the moisture from the top of the eggplant slices. Turn them over, sprinkle the second side with salt, using about ½ teaspoon, and let stand for another 20 minutes. Blot the moisture from the second side of the eggplant slices. Let stand while preparing the tomato sauce.

Place a perforated stainless-steel grill pan on the grill and preheat the grill to between medium and medium-high heat (350°F–375°F). Brush the salted eggplant slices with olive oil on both sides. Grill the eggplant, turning once, until browned in spots and very tender, about 4 minutes per side (the grilling time will vary with heat and will be shorter if you're not using a grill pan).

Preheat the oven to 375°F. Line the bottom of a large oval baking dish (mine is about 14½ x 10 inches) or a 13 x 9 x 2-inch rectangular baking dish with half of the grilled eggplant slices, overlapping slightly. Spoon about one third of the tomato sauce over the eggplant slices, using more if you like it extra saucy (you might or might not need the entire recipe of sauce).

Sprinkle half of the mozzarella and half of the Parmesan over the sauce. Top with the remaining eggplant, another one third (or more) of the sauce, the remaining mozzarella, and then the remaining Parmesan cheese. Cover the dish tightly with foil and bake until the sauce is bubbling and the dish is heated through, about 25 minutes.

Uncover and bake until the cheeses are melted and bubbling and the sauce bubbles vigorously, about 8 minutes longer. Remove from the oven, sprinkle with the fresh basil, and let stand for 10 minutes before serving.

WINE: Flat Creek Estate has produced a wonderful Sangiovese-based red wine for years—and it's one of the best Italian-style wines in the state. Look for the Super Texan, a medium-bodied red with balanced acid and spices.

BEER: With toasted malt flavors and a balanced, clean finish, an India pale ale, such as Pedernales Classic IPA, is a lovely quaffer with Italian dishes like this.

Double-Crust Creamy Mushroom Pie

Our longtime friends Ethan Sperry and Siri Hoogen are among my favorite people to share a meal with: We lived in Los Angeles at the same time and we wound up in Ohio for several years together, too. Siri made this savory pie, which was featured in, naturally, *Bon Appétit* (I've since adapted it), as a vegetarian offering for Thanksgiving. On the subject of large quantities of mushrooms, any cooking class will teach you that you're not supposed to wash fresh mushrooms—they're like sponges and absorb water so you're just supposed to brush off or wipe off any dirt. But I'll admit that I wash my mushrooms every time. (I know what they grow in, and I know I can cook off that extra water much more easily than I can get over my need to wash them.) I make this in a deep-dish ceramic pie dish that's 9 inches in diameter; it would also work in a shallower 9- to 10-inch glass pie dish.

Makes about 8 servings

Savory Double Crust (page 116)

Unbleached all-purpose flour, for rolling

3 tablespoons extra-virgin olive oil

1 large onion, chopped (about 3 cups)

2 pounds cremini mushrooms, washed, drained, and coarsely chopped

2 tablespoons fresh thyme leaves

1 (8-ounce package) cream cheese or Neufchâtel cheese

Kosher salt and freshly ground black pepper

1 large egg, beaten

Prepare the dough for the Savory Double Crust (page 116). Divide the dough into two disks, using one third of the dough for a smaller disk and two thirds of the dough for a larger disk.

Line a work surface with a large square of parchment paper. Sprinkle it with unbleached flour, then place the larger dough disk on the parchment and sprinkle the dough lightly with flour. Roll the dough into a 13-inch-diameter round. Invert the dough into a 9-inch pie dish, carefully peeling off the parchment. Using a fork, prick the bottom of the crust a few times.

Sprinkle the parchment paper with flour again and roll out the smaller disk to a 10-inch-diameter round. Leave the dough round on the parchment paper, place it atop the dough-lined pie dish, and chill both while preparing the filling.

Preheat the oven to 400°F. Heat the extra-virgin olive oil in a large, heavy skillet over medium-high heat. Add the onion and sauté until tender and translucent, about 5 minutes. Add the mushrooms and thyme and sauté until the mushroom juices are released, the liquid cooks off, and the mushrooms begin to brown, 15 to 20 minutes (it will take less time in a very large skillet). Turn the heat off.

Chop the cheese into large chunks and add it to the skillet, stirring gently until the cheese melts and is incorporated into the filling. Season to taste with salt and pepper.

Remove the crusts from the refrigerator. Fill the bottom crust with the warm mushroom filling. Top with the smaller crust, trimming the sides if necessary and crimping the edges to seal. Using a sharp knife, slice five or six vent holes in the top crust, radiating out from the center. Using a pastry brush, brush the top crust with the beaten egg. Bake the pie until the crust is golden brown and baked through and the filling is hot, about 30 minutes. Let it cool at least 15 minutes. Serve warm.

Savory Double Crust

This simple recipe turns out a deliciously flaky, thick crust that rises just a bit. I use it rolled into two rounds for the Double-Crust Creamy Mushroom Pie (page 114), as well as rolled into one big rectangle atop the Old-Fashioned Vegetable Pot Pie (page 124). While I often make it with yogurt, I've also prepared a vegan version by replacing the yogurt with cashew cream; the dairy version is a bit fluffier, but it's delicious either way.

Makes 1 double crust :: **Vegan Option**

1½ cups unbleached all-purpose flour, plus more flour for rolling

¼ cup plus 2 tablespoons white whole wheat flour

1½ teaspoons baking powder

¾ teaspoon salt (skip if using vegan butter)

6 ounces (1½ sticks) cold unsalted butter or vegan butter sticks (such as Earth Balance), coarsely chopped

¾ cup plain Greek yogurt or plain 2% or low-fat yogurt, or (for vegan) Basic Cashew Cream (page 96)

In a large bowl, whisk the flours and baking powder to blend. Rub the cold butter or vegan butter into the flour mixture with your fingertips until incorporated (do not overwork). Using a fork, stir in the yogurt or cashew cream. Knead gently until the dough comes together. Wrap it in plastic wrap and chill until ready to use.

Can be prepared up to a day ahead.

WINE: An easy-drinking red, such as "Cornelious" Tempranillo from Inwood Estates, is just what these mushrooms need.

BEER: The Brewhouse Brown Ale from Real Ale Brewing is rich and delicious, and it loves hearty foods, such as this mushroom pie, to pair with.

Black Bean Soft Tacos with Salsa and Shredded Lettuce

||||||||||||||||||||||||||||||||||||||||||||||||||||||||||||||||||||||||||||||||||||||||||||||||

Tender corn tortillas wrapped around perfectly spiced beans, from-scratch salsa, and feathery shredded lettuce will make you feel sorry for people who think tacos are only made with beef. These can be customized to suit any tastes. For a change from black beans, try filling them with Garlicky Pinto Beans (page 76) and Fresh Tomato, Corn, and Pepper Salsa (page 22). These little tacos are gluten-free and easy to keep vegan, too, if you use the Guacamole with Tomato and Cilantro (page 20) instead of the queso fresco. Plan on up to three tacos per person.

Serves 6 to 8 :: **Vegan Option • GF**

Black Beans Simmered with Onion and Jalapeño (page 118)

Restaurant-Style Smoky Red Salsa (page 23), or any favorite purchased salsa

½ large head fresh romaine lettuce

½ 10-ounce round queso fresco or (for vegan) Guacamole with Tomato and Cilantro (page 20) (optional)

About 6 tablespoons canola oil, divided

18 small corn tortillas (gluten-free, if desired; for homemade, see page 173)

WINE: Zinfandel has a snappy kick that goes down well with lots of Mexican-style dishes. Becker Vineyards Zinfandel delivers a bit of raspberry and mocha flavors, too.

BEER: A straightforward—but still very flavorful—ale, like the 1st Street Ale from No Label Brewing Co., complements these tacos with a smooth taste and a clean ending.

Prepare the black beans. Prepare the salsa and transfer it to a serving bowl.

Fit a food processor with the shredding blade, and finely shred the romaine lettuce (or slice it very thinly by hand), then transfer it to a serving bowl. Crumble the queso fresco, if using, into a small serving bowl, or place the guacamole in a serving bowl.

If the tortillas are too crumbly to wrap around taco fillings (most store-bought ones are), heat them up: Heat 1 teaspoon of oil in a small, heavy skillet over medium-high heat. Add one tortilla at a time and cook, turning once, until the tortilla softens and is heated all the way through, about 1 minute. Repeat with the remaining tortillas and oil.

Spoon about ¼ cup of the black beans into the center of each tortilla and serve immediately, passing salsa, lettuce, and queso fresco or guacamole, if desired, separately.

Black Beans Simmered with Onion and Jalapeño

Homemade beans have a better taste and texture than canned. That's why every cook needs a go-to recipe for black beans from scratch. This one is nicely seasoned, and it yields a big pot of beans that make a great side dish on their own, and also are excellent in soft tacos (see page 117) or simply ladled over individual bowls of rice (such as the Cilantro-Lime Texas Basmati, page 161). When you're seasoning the beans, keep in mind that smoked paprika lends a mild smoky flavor, whereas chipotle chili powder lends more heat. The cooking time will vary depending on the freshness of the beans and how long you're able to soak them beforehand.

Makes about 7 cups beans :: **V • GF**

1 pound dried black beans

2 tablespoons plus 1½ teaspoons kosher salt, divided

2 tablespoons extra-virgin olive oil

1 large white or yellow onion, chopped

3 large jalapeño peppers, seeded and chopped

4 garlic cloves, peeled and chopped

2 teaspoons ground cumin

½ teaspoon smoked paprika or chipotle chili powder, or more to taste

Place the beans in a colander and rinse well, picking out any that are shriveled or otherwise unappetizing. Transfer the beans to a large, heavy pot, stir in 2 tablespoons salt and enough water to cover beans by 2 inches, cover, and soak for at least 6 hours and up to overnight. Drain the beans in the colander, rinsing well.

In a large, heavy pot, heat the oil over medium-high heat. Add the onion and sauté until tender and translucent, about 5 minutes. Add the jalapeños and sauté for 2 minutes longer. Add the garlic and sauté just until fragrant, about 1 minute. Stir in the cumin. Add 6 cups of water and the beans, cover, increase the heat to high, and bring to a boil. Lower the heat to low and simmer gently until the beans are tender, anywhere from 45 minutes to 1½ hours. Season to taste with the remaining 1½ teaspoons of salt, or more to taste, and smoked paprika. Serve warm.

Can be prepared ahead. Let cool, then cover and refrigerate for up to 3 days. Bring to a simmer before serving.

White Cheddar–Green Chile Mac and Cheese

This recipe comes from Michele Head's sister, Jessica Haynes, who lives near San Antonio and who I've had the pleasure of cooking with both on camping trips and in the kitchen. This dish is ridiculously rich, but a small serving alongside a big green salad balances it out nicely, or try it as a side dish for anything from the grill. If you like a crusty top, it can be transferred to a baking dish, topped with more cheese, and baked (this is more traditional but comes out less creamy) or better yet, briefly broiled. Otherwise, serve it creamy and hot, straight from the pot.

Makes 4 to 6 servings

8 ounces elbow macaroni noodles (ridged if you can find them)

2 tablespoons unsalted butter

2 tablespoons unbleached all-purpose flour

1½ cups whole milk or half-and-half

½ cup chopped freshly roasted green chiles, or 1 (4-ounce) can chopped green chiles

10 ounces mixed cheeses (I use sharp white Cheddar and Monterey Jack), grated (about 4 cups total)

Sea salt and freshly ground black pepper

RECIPE CONTINUES

Cook the pasta in a large, heavy pot of boiling salted water until tender but slightly on the al dente side. Drain in a colander; set aside.

In the same large, heavy pot used for the pasta, melt the butter over medium heat. Whisk in the flour and cook until the roux is bubbling (it should be light in color), about 2 minutes. Add the milk, whisking constantly. Increase the heat to medium-high and whisk until the sauce thickens and just begins to bubble around the edges.

Whisk in the chiles and cook until heated through and the mixture just begins to bubble again. Remove from the heat. If you're planning to broil or bake the macaroni and cheese, set aside ½ cup of the cheese. Add the remaining cheese to the sauce, a handful at a time, whisking until melted. Add the pasta and stir to coat. Season to taste with salt and pepper. Serve immediately if you don't plan to broil or bake it.

If broiling, arrange the oven rack in the middle of the oven and preheat the broiler. Transfer the macaroni and cheese to 2-quart ceramic baking dish. Sprinkle with the reserved ½ cup of cheese, and broil until the cheese melts and just begins to brown in spots, 2 to 3 minutes (alternatively, bake it at 350°F until the cheese melts and the sauce is bubbling, about 25 minutes). Serve warm.

WINE: A white wine with a lot of flavor is needed here. McPherson Cellars Roussanne is just the kind to do the job. It's aromatic and loaded with herbaceous and citrus notes to cut through the richness.

BEER: Live Oak Big Bark Amber Lager delivers the kind of malty flavor that harmonizes with the deep Cheddar.

Grilled Tofu Steaks with Sweet and Spicy Barbecue Sauce

//

This simple main course was inspired by a dish I used to order at the now-defunct Zen Grill in Los Angeles, where a mouth-searingly spicy barbecued tofu steak was served with a side of skinny green beans. I never got the restaurant's recipe, but Texans' love of barbecue inspired me to revisit the idea. My sauce has a kick but is more family-friendly than its inspiration (adjust the heat up or down with more or less chipotle). If you're in a hurry, sub in your favorite bottled sauce. My kids and husband think this tofu tastes like barbecued chicken; I do not. In short, everyone's happy when grilled tofu steaks are on the dinner menu.

Makes about 4 servings; doubles easily :: **V • GF**

2 (14-ounce) packages organic firm tofu, or
2 (12-ounce) packages organic extra-firm

Sweet and Spicy Barbecue Sauce (page 123)

Line a large dinner plate or cutting board with a clean dish towel. Drain both slabs of tofu, rinse, pat dry, and place on the towel-lined plate or cutting board. Wrap the ends of the dish towel over the tofu to cover completely. Top with a second dinner plate or cutting board, and add two or three cans (or similar weight) to press the tofu. Let it stand for at least 45 minutes and up to 2 hours.

Remove the tofu from the dish towel. Slice each slab in half crosswise, so each slab is divided into two thinner slabs. Cut each thin slab diagonally in half, forming a total of eight large triangles. Place the tofu triangles on a large platter. Brush liberally with the barbecue sauce, turning once, to completely cover each triangle with sauce. Let stand for 30 minutes to marinate.

Place a perforated stainless-steel grill topper (see sidebar, page 105) on the grill. Preheat the grill to 400°F. Add the tofu to the grill pan and grill, turning once, until the tofu is heated through and the edges become crisp, about 4 minutes per side. (Alternatively, to bake the tofu, preheat the oven to 425°F. Line a baking dish with parchment paper. Bake the tofu until heated through and the edges begin to crisp, about 30 minutes.) Transfer the grilled or baked tofu to a serving platter. Brush with the sauce again and serve warm, passing additional sauce separately.

Sweet and Spicy Barbecue Sauce

This versatile sauce makes more than enough for the tofu recipe. It's also great in vegetarian baked beans (see page 171), and would be delicious on grilled portobello mushrooms, too (see page 127).

Makes about 1½ cups sauce :: **V • GF**

1 tablespoon extra-virgin olive oil

1 tablespoon minced fresh ginger (from about a 1-inch length of peeled fresh ginger)

2 garlic cloves, peeled and minced

1 cup ketchup

¼ cup packed organic dark brown sugar

¼ cup tamari

¼ cup freshly squeezed lemon juice

1 whole chipotle chile in adobo sauce (from a 7-ounce can; gluten-free, if desired), minced (leave the seeds in)

Heat the olive oil in a small, heavy saucepan over medium heat. Add the ginger and garlic and sauté just until fragrant and beginning to soften, about 30 seconds. Whisk in the ketchup, brown sugar, tamari, lemon juice, and chipotle chile. Bring the sauce to a boil, then lower the heat to medium-low, cover, and simmer until thick and syrupy, about 10 minutes.

Can be prepared up to 2 days ahead of time. Let cool, then cover and refrigerate. Rewarm before serving.

WINE: There are many red wine choices to consider here (such as Tempranillo, Syrah, and Zinfandel) but the best flavor-pairings would be produced with a Malbec, like the one from Haak Vineyards & Winery.

BEER: Tofu will stand up to a full-bodied beer—at least if it has this sweet and spicy sauce. (512) Brewing Company's Pecan Porter is easy to drink for being such a big beer. And it plays very nicely with food.

CHIPOTLE CHILES

If they look like a familiar size and shape, that's because chipotle chiles are just jalapeño peppers that have been smoked. The canned variety—packed in a vinegary tomato sauce called adobo—is used in several recipes in this book to add heat, smoke, and depth to dishes. (Likewise, chipotle chili powder offers much more heat and smokiness than standard chili powder.) Chipotle chiles in adobo sauce are sold in 7-ounce cans; some brands are gluten-free but others are not. A little goes a long way—that one can could be used in half a dozen recipes or more. Transfer any leftovers to a glass container, cover, and refrigerate for up to a week or two. Alternatively, chipotle chiles may be frozen in an airtight container for months.

Old-Fashioned Vegetable Pot Pie

This homespun casserole is pure comfort food for all ages; serve it with a crisp green salad and brown rice to help soak up any of the extra juices. To prepare the vegan version, you'll need one recipe of Basic Cashew Cream (page 96); part of it will be used in the crust and part in the filling.

Makes about 8 servings :: **Vegan Option**

Savory Double Crust (page 116)

2 tablespoons unsalted butter or vegan butter (such as Earth Balance)

1 large yellow onion, chopped (about 3 cups)

8 ounces cremini mushrooms, trimmed and coarsely chopped

1½ pounds Yukon Gold potatoes (about 5 medium-size potatoes), chopped into ½-inch pieces

1 medium-size sweet potato (about 10 ounces), peeled and chopped into ½-inch pieces

8 ounces carrots (about 3 large carrots), peeled and sliced diagonally into ⅓- to ½-inch-thick slices

1 tablespoon unbleached all-purpose flour

1 tablespoon chopped fresh rosemary

1 tablespoon fresh thyme leaves, or 1 teaspoon dried

1½ teaspoons kosher salt

¼ teaspoon freshly ground black pepper

2 cups frozen sweet peas (about 9 ounces)

½ cup heavy whipping cream or (for vegan) Basic Cashew Cream (page 96)

1 large egg, beaten, or 3 tablespoons extra-virgin olive oil

Prepare the crust; pat the dough into one large ball, cover with plastic wrap, and chill until needed.

Melt the butter or vegan butter in a large, heavy pot over medium-high heat; add the onion and sauté until tender and translucent, about 5 minutes. Add the mushrooms and sauté until the mushrooms release their juices and just begin to brown in spots, about 5 minutes.

Stir in the potatoes, sweet potato, and carrots. Sprinkle with the flour, rosemary, thyme, salt, and pepper and stir. Stir in 3 cups of water, cover, and bring to a boil. Lower the heat to medium-low and simmer until the vegetables are just tender, about 10 minutes. Stir in the peas and cream or cashew cream and bring to a boil. Remove from the heat. Season to taste with additional salt and pepper, if desired. Transfer the mixture to a 13 x 9 x 2-inch casserole dish.

Preheat the oven to 400°F. Line a work surface with a rectangle of parchment paper; sprinkle the parchment with flour. Roll the dough out to a 13 x 9-inch rectangle. Roll the dough rectangle loosely around the rolling pin to transfer it to the top of the casserole; unroll the dough over the casserole, trimming any excess dough off the edges. Using a sharp knife, slash vent holes in the dough.

Using a pastry brush, brush the dough lightly with the beaten egg or the olive oil. Immediately transfer the casserole to the oven and bake until the crust is golden and puffed and the vegetable mixture is bubbling and hot, about 30 minutes. Let stand for 15 minutes. Serve warm.

WINE: Because we don't grow the Austrian grape Grüner Veltliner in Texas, the next-best wine to serve here would be an herbal Chenin Blanc, such as that from McPherson Cellars. It's versatile, it's got great acidity, and it's got divine minerality.

BEER: The Texas Big Beer Brewery makes Working Stiff Ale, which is a very flavorful beer that will enhance the vegetable flavors here, but will also stay out of the way when it needs to.

PLT (Portobello-Lettuce-Tomato) Sandwiches

Summer's favorite sandwich is easy to make vegetarian and even vegan: Replace the traditional bacon with Grilled Portobello Steak Strips (page 127), and slather on some smoky chipotle mayonnaise to contribute to the classic flavor profile.

Makes 4 :: **Vegan Option**

¼ cup mayonnaise or vegan mayonnaise (such as Vegenaise)

1 whole chipotle chile in adobo sauce (from a 7-ounce can), finely minced (leave the seeds in)

Grilled Portobello Steak Strips (page 127)

4 (4 x 5-inch) ciabatta or torta rolls, or 8 large slices rustic whole-grain bread (vegan, if desired)

2 tablespoons extra-virgin olive oil

2 medium-size tomatoes (about 6 ounces total), thinly sliced

2 cups loosely packed fresh baby greens (spring mix, spinach, chard, kale, or any combination)

1 large, ripe avocado, peeled and pitted

In a small bowl, whisk the mayonnaise or vegan mayonnaise and chipotle chile to blend.

Preheat the grill and then grill the portobello mushrooms according to the Grilled Portobello Steak Strips recipe instructions, leaving the grill on for the bread.

Brush the cut sides of the torta rolls with the olive oil. Grill the rolls, cut side down, until lightly toasted and grill marks just begin to show, about 1½ minutes.

Spread the bottom half of the rolls generously with the chipotle mayonnaise. Top with the portobello strips. Top the mushrooms with the tomato slices, and then the fresh baby greens, dividing equally.

Cut the avocado into quarters and spread one quarter of the avocado over the top half of each roll. Close the sandwiches and cut in half. Serve warm or at room temperature.

WINE: A medium- to full-bodied Merlot, such as that from William Chris Vineyards, is a deep and complex red that doesn't hit a bad note when paired with this sandwich.

BEER: Belgian-style ales seem to be brewed just for picnics. So when serving these sandwiches, the Lucky Ol' Sun from Ranger Creek Brewing & Distilling would be a smart choice.

COCKTAIL: Try the Sangria Rosa (page 215), especially when inviting a crowd.

MEATLESS IN COWTOWN

Grilled Portobello Steak Strips

Rich, meaty-tasting portobello mushrooms, grilled and sliced into steaklike strips, make a great main course on their own and in a sandwich (see the PLT recipe, page 126). Atop a green salad, they make it hearty enough for a main course (for recipes, see pages 73–132).

4 servings :: **V • GF**

4 large portobello mushrooms (at least 12 ounces total)

¼ cup extra-virgin olive oil

2 tablespoons balsamic vinegar

2 garlic cloves, peeled and minced

½ teaspoon kosher salt

¼ teaspoon freshly ground black pepper

Remove the mushroom stems and use a spoon to scrape out the mushroom gills, if desired. Wash the mushrooms, then let them dry on a clean kitchen towel.

In a small bowl, whisk the oil, vinegar, garlic, salt, and pepper to blend. Place the mushrooms on a large plate or platter. Using a pastry brush, brush the mushrooms all over with the oil and vinegar mixture. Let stand, rounded side down, for 30 minutes to 1 hour to marinate.

Meanwhile, preheat the grill to medium-high (about 375°F).

Place the mushrooms on the preheated grill, rounded side down. Grill the mushrooms until they are tender and juicy and grill marks show, turning once, 4 to 5 minutes per side. Transfer them to a cutting board and slice into ¼- to ½-inch-thick strips. Serve warm or at room temperature.

WINE: The Malbec grape, though originally from France, thrives in Argentina—and Texas. The deep red Malbec from Torre di Pietra is bold and great for grilled foods.

BEER: I like pairing smoke with meat (so to speak). The smoky Pecan Porter from (512) Brewing Company is deep and rich enough to stand up to the meaty flavors of the mushrooms here.

Tamale Pie with Black Beans and Sweet Potato

I have occasionally made real tamales from scratch, but I don't necessarily recommend it. Unless you have access to fresh masa or the season's sweetest, freshest, corn, the results don't always justify the effort, especially considering that you can pick up prepared tamales from local markets (look for versions not made with lard). A tamale pie—chili-scented veggies topped with a sweet corn crust—is a different story, however, and can be pulled off any night of the week. Some versions are topped with cornbread, whereas others are topped with polenta. This one is somewhere in between—more, well, tamale-like. If using stone-ground cornmeal, look for a finely ground version for this dish.

Makes about 8 servings :: **V • GF**

Vegetable Filling

2 tablespoons extra-virgin olive oil

1 medium-size white or yellow onion, finely chopped (about 2 cups)

2 medium-size jalapeño peppers, seeded and minced

2 garlic cloves, peeled and minced

1 medium-size sweet potato, peeled and cut into ½-inch pieces (about 8 ounces, or 1½ cups)

¾ cup fresh corn kernels (from 1 ear of corn) or frozen corn kernels

½ teaspoon ground cumin

½ teaspoon chili powder

½ teaspoon garlic powder (gluten-free, if desired)

1 (14.5-ounce) can fire-roasted diced tomatoes (with or without green chiles)

1¾ cups prepared black beans, or 1 (15-ounce can) black beans, drained

½ cup loosely packed fresh cilantro leaves, chopped

Salt (optional)

Corn Topping

1 cup finely ground cornmeal

½ cup masa harina

2 tablespoons organic granulated sugar

2 teaspoons baking powder

½ teaspoon salt

½ cup canola oil

1½ cups fresh corn kernels (from 2 ears of corn) or frozen corn kernels, coarsely chopped

½ cup loosely packed fresh cilantro leaves, chopped

RECIPE CONTINUES ▶

To make the vegetable filling: Heat the olive oil in a medium, heavy pot over medium-high heat. Add the onion and sauté until tender and translucent, about 5 minutes. Add the jalapeños and garlic and sauté until fragrant and tender, about 1 minute. Add the sweet potato and corn and sauté 3 minutes. Stir in the cumin, chili powder, and garlic powder. Stir in the tomatoes, beans, and 1 cup of water.

Cover the pot and bring to a boil, then lower the heat to medium-low and simmer, covered, until the sweet potatoes are just tender (they should not be mushy), about 15 minutes. Remove from the heat. Stir in the cilantro. Season to taste with salt, if desired.

Transfer the vegetable filling to a 13 x 9 x 2-inch glass baking dish.

To make the corn topping: Preheat the oven to 375°F.

In a large bowl, whisk the cornmeal, masa harina, sugar, baking powder, and salt to blend. Stir in the oil. Add 1 cup of water and whisk to blend. Fold in the corn and cilantro.

Spoon the mixture over the vegetable filling evenly and bake uncovered until the corn topping is baked through (a knife inserted into the center comes out clean) and the vegetable filling is bubbling, 30 to 35 minutes. Serve warm.

WINE: Texas Tempranillo is the best wine for this hearty tamale pie because the flavors are practically seamless. Pedernales Cellars makes Tempranillo from the Hill Country that delivers bright plum, earth, and smoke flavors.

BEER: Rahr & Sons brews a wonderful red lager, Rahr's Red, which will pick up the savory black bean flavors and run with them.

Cashew-Quinoa Patties

This recipe comes from Amy McNutt of Spiral Diner & Bakery, a beloved vegan restaurant right here in Fort Worth (read more on page 133). These patties are seriously delicious; the mixture is similar in texture to risotto, and they are pretty tender after cooking, too. Serve them on a bun with your favorite burger fixings, or just alongside some mashed potatoes and veggies. Amy recommends the same brand that I love for broth: Rapunzel Vegan Vegetable Bouillon. It has a wonderful herb flavor and is widely available; for this recipe, use one cube dissolved in 2½ cups of water. Nutritional yeast can be found in health foods stores; it gives vegan foods a cheesy flavor.

Makes ten 4-inch patties :: **V • GF**

2½ cups vegan vegetable stock

1 cup organic white quinoa

¼ cup plus 2 tablespoons vegetable oil

1 medium-size yellow onion, chopped (about 2 cups)

2 tablespoons minced garlic (from about 8 garlic cloves)

1 cup raw cashews, divided

½ cup shredded carrot (from about 1 large carrot, peeled)

¼ cup tapioca starch or tapioca flour

¼ cup chopped fresh flat-leaf parsley leaves, or 2 tablespoons dried

2 tablespoons nutritional yeast

1¾ teaspoons baking powder

1 teaspoon freshly ground black pepper

½ teaspoon kosher salt

RECIPE CONTINUES

Combine the stock and quinoa in a small, heavy saucepan. Cover and bring to a boil. Lower the heat to low and simmer, covered, until all of the liquid is absorbed, 25 to 30 minutes.

Preheat the oven to 300°F.

Heat the oil in a medium, heavy skillet over medium-high heat. Add the onion and garlic and cook, stirring frequently, until the onion and garlic are soft and translucent, 5 to 7 minutes. Set aside.

Using a blender or food processor, combine ½ cup of the cashews with ¾ cup of water; blend until smooth. Coarsely chop the remaining ½ cup of cashews.

In a large bowl, combine the blended and chopped cashews, cooked quinoa, onion mixture, and all the remaining ingredients. Using a rubber spatula, mix until thoroughly combined.

Line a baking sheet with parchment paper. Using a ½-cup measure, scoop ½ cup of the mixture and turn it out onto the prepared baking sheet, spacing apart like cookies (about five will fit on a baking sheet). Bake until the tops of the patties are beginning to look dry, about 25 minutes. Using a spatula, carefully flip the patties over (they will still be very soft and tender), and bake on the second side for an additional 25 minutes. Serve warm.

The patties can be prepared ahead of time. Bake, then let cool, cover, and refrigerate. Just before serving, heat 1 tablespoon of oil in a large, heavy nonstick skillet. Cook up to three patties at a time, turning once, until lightly browned on both sides and heated through, about 5 minutes total.

WINE: A simply flavored white wine, such as Three Dudes Chenin Blanc, allows the flavors of this dish to stay untrammeled.

BEER: Karbach Brewing Co.'s Weisse Versa Wheat is a deliciously crisp wheat beer with mouth-filling banana, citrus, and warm spices. Wheat beers similar to this would bring out some wonderful cashew flavors for the dish.

VEGAN IN COWTOWN

Spiral Diner & Bakery celebrated a decade in 2012, which is no small feat in the restaurant world. And for this completely vegan restaurant that got its start in a city that refers to itself as "Cowtown," it's an especially sweet milestone (there's a location in Dallas now, too). With a menu of comfort foods made vegan, Amy McNutt and James Johnston attract a diverse crowd of vegans, vegetarians, and omnivores who appreciate a clean meal. Everyone from diet-conscious athletes to those who keep kosher know they're in good hands. And as anyone who's vegan or vegetarian knows, it's an unusually liberating feeling to find yourself sitting in a restaurant where you can enjoy *everything* on the menu—no questions to be asked. The wife-and-husband team has since turned over operations to Lindsey Akey in Fort Worth and Sara Tomerlin in Dallas. At press time, Amy was in the fundraising phase of opening the Citizen Theater, which will be Fort Worth's first devoted art house movie theater. James is focusing on a burgeoning film career (he produced *Ain't Them Bodies Saints* and *Listen Up Philip*, among others). But they still make time to develop new recipes for the pair of restaurants, including the Cashew-Quinoa Patties she shared with us (page 131).

BREAKFAST

It's the most important meal of the day, and it's probably the best-loved one, as well. That's why about once a week, we have breakfast food for both breakfast *and* dinner. Although weekday mornings might call for a quick bowl of granola with a handful of berries, weekends and evenings usually mean waffles or pancakes or quiche. This special section also includes our favorite quick breads; these loaves and muffins can be stirred up quickly, baked, and enjoyed any time of day, though they are especially good with a cup of coffee.

Nutty Coconut Granola

Lightly sweetened with maple syrup, this granola skips the cloying sweetness of so many commercially sold versions. It's also a great breakfast treat to bring as a hostess gift when staying overnight with friends or family. After baking, toss in some dried fruit—cranberries, mangoes, blueberries—or better yet, serve it with fresh peaches, bananas, raspberries, or blackberries. Granola is traditionally enjoyed at room temperature, but anyone lucky enough to be hanging around the kitchen when it comes out of the oven should indulge in a warm bowl with cool milk.

Makes about 5 cups granola :: **V • GF**

3 cups old-fashioned rolled oats (gluten-free, if desired)

½ cup coarsely chopped pecans

½ cup coarsely chopped walnuts

½ cup raw pepitas or sunflower seeds

½ cup unsweetened shredded coconut or sweetened shredded coconut

¼ cup raw golden flaxseeds (optional)

1 teaspoon ground cinnamon

½ teaspoon kosher salt

½ cup pure maple syrup

½ cup coconut oil or canola oil

1 tablespoon vanilla extract

Preheat the oven to 300°F. Line a 13 x 9 x 2-inch glass baking dish with parchment paper.

Combine the oats, nuts, pepitas, coconut, flaxseeds, if using, cinnamon, and salt in a large bowl; toss to mix well. Heat the syrup, oil, and vanilla in a small, heavy saucepan over medium-low heat, stirring just until the syrup thins and the mixture is heated through, about 2 minutes. Pour the hot syrup mixture over the oat mixture; using a rubber spatula, fold the syrup into the dry ingredients until they are evenly moistened.

Transfer the oat mixture to the prepared baking dish and bake, stirring occasionally, until the granola is lightly browned and fragrant and the nuts are toasted, about 45 minutes. Let cool, then store in an airtight container at room temperature.

Can be prepared up to 1 week ahead.

Texas Grapefruit Brûlée

Compared to spring's slender asparagus stalks and summer's luscious tomatoes, wintertime produce is sometimes overlooked. But here in Texas, cooler months mean an abundance of Ruby Red and Rio Star grapefruit. While we usually just eat grapefruit as they are—naturally sweet enough that only the children add any sugar—this dressed-up version is fun when company's coming. In addition to its obvious breakfast and brunch appeal, it also makes a good dessert, particularly if served alongside biscotti or shortbread. A handheld butane torch makes short work of this presentation (and it gives you an excuse to use it for something other than crème brûlée), but it's also possible to caramelize the sugar under a broiler.

Serves 4 :: **V • GF**

2 large Texas red grapefruit, such as Rio Star or Ruby Sweet

About 8 teaspoons coarse turbinado sugar or organic granulated sugar

If you don't have a handheld butane torch, preheat the broiler. Halve each grapefruit crosswise, and remove any visible seeds. Using a sharp paring knife, slice between each membrane and around the edge to loosen the grapefruit segments.

Using a paper towel or clean kitchen towel, gently blot juice from the top of each grapefruit half. Sprinkle each grapefruit half evenly with 1 to 2 teaspoons of sugar (depending on the size of the fruit), covering the fruit completely with a thin layer of sugar.

Using a handheld kitchen torch, heat the sugar atop each grapefruit until it melts, bubbles, and begins to turn light brown in spots, about 30 seconds each. (Alternatively, arrange the grapefruit halves on a rimmed baking sheet and broil until the sugar is melted, bubbly, and browning in spots, about 3 minutes.) Transfer the grapefruit halves to the refrigerator to chill until the caramelized sugar cools and hardens, about 10 minutes. Can be prepared up to 1 hour ahead; keep chilled until ready to serve.

Rosemary- and Sage-Roasted Potatoes and Peppers

Who doesn't love potatoes at breakfast time, lunchtime, or dinnertime? Roasting vegetables works best when the pan isn't crowded: Spread this out between two parchment paper–lined baking dishes to produce those enviable browned edges.

Makes 6 to 8 side-dish servings :: **V** • **GF**

2 pounds Yukon Gold potatoes, scrubbed, cut into ½- to ¾-inch chunks

½ large sweet onion, coarsely chopped (about 1½ cups)

1 large red bell pepper, stemmed, seeded, and coarsely chopped (about 1 cup)

1 large poblano chile, stemmed, seeded, and coarsely chopped (about 1 cup)

1 tablespoon minced fresh rosemary

1 tablespoon minced fresh sage

1 teaspoon kosher salt

¼ cup extra-virgin olive oil

Preheat the oven to 450°F. Line two large baking dishes with parchment paper.

Place the potatoes, onion, bell pepper, and chile in a large bowl. Sprinkle the herbs and salt over the vegetables. Drizzle with the olive oil and, using your hands, toss to coat. Divide the vegetables between the prepared baking dishes, spreading out in a single layer. Roast the vegetables until they are tender all the way through and beginning to brown on the edges, stirring occasionally after about 20 minutes, 45 to 50 minutes total. Serve warm or at room temperature.

Better-Than-Classic Waffles

Like many kids in the '70s, I grew up eating waffles with Log Cabin "maple" syrup, but after our Ohio friends John and Julie Wilcox began tapping their maple trees and cooking the sap down, doling out small, dear bottles of good-enough-to-be-illicit syrup, there was no turning back. This recipe has both traditional and vegan options, and it's hard to say which is better. The vegan version comes out a little lighter in color and crispier in texture, but it has more of a tendency to stick, so be sure brush the waffle iron with oil first and let vegan waffles cook slightly longer. We have these every weekend, and often make peanut butter sandwiches out of the leftover waffles to pack in school lunches the next day.

Makes about 6 servings :: **Vegan Option**

1½ cups unbleached all-purpose flour

¾ cup whole wheat flour or white whole wheat flour

2 tablespoons organic granulated sugar

1 tablespoon baking powder

½ teaspoon kosher salt

2¼ cups milk or (for vegan) unsweetened almond milk

½ cup canola oil, plus more for waffle iron

2 large eggs or (for vegan) flax eggs (page 141)

Fresh fruit, such as mixed berries, sliced peaches, or sliced bananas

Toasted nuts, such as slivered almonds, pecans, or walnuts

Pure maple syrup

In a large mixing bowl, combine the flours, sugar, baking powder, and salt; whisk to blend. In a medium mixing bowl, combine the milk, oil, and eggs or flax eggs, whisking to blend well.

Preheat the waffle iron; using a pastry brush, coat it lightly with vegetable oil. Add the wet ingredients to the dry ingredients and whisk to combine well.

Using a soup ladle, pour some batter into the center of the preheated waffle iron, close it, and bake the waffle until it's just cooked through, 2 to 3 minutes. Repeat with the remaining batter. Serve the waffles hot with fresh fruit, toasted nuts, and maple syrup.

Flax Eggs

I love a work-around that's inexpensive, wholesome, and delicious. Homemade flax "eggs" (an egg replacement simply made with ground raw golden flaxseeds and water) can be all three. It only takes a few seconds in a countertop coffee or spice grinder to turn those golden seeds into a fragrant powder. It's best to keep your flaxseeds whole until you need them, for both spoilage and health reasons; if you want to keep flaxseed meal on hand, be sure to freeze it. You can't scramble flax eggs, but their nutty flavor is right at home in waffles (see page 140) and in many cookie recipes, too (starting on page 189).

Replaces 1 large egg : : **V • GF**

1 tablespoon freshly ground raw golden
   flaxseeds

3 tablespoons warm water

Mix the ground flaxseeds with the warm water; let stand for a few minutes to gel. Use as directed in the recipes (doubling or tripling as needed) to replace eggs in waffles, pancakes, cookies, quick breads, and more.

Spinach, Cheese, and Ciabatta Brunch Strata

Ever so slowly, Anthony's appetite for sweet breakfast foods has evolved to favor savory dishes. This strata that he and Michele make is a very satisfying morning meal and a regular dish whenever they host overnight guests. Be sure to start preparing it the night before to give the bread enough time to soak up all the liquid.

Makes 6 to 8 servings

1 (10-ounce) package frozen spinach, thawed

3 tablespoons unsalted butter

1 medium-size sweet onion, finely chopped (about 2 cups)

1 teaspoon salt, divided

½ teaspoon freshly ground black pepper, divided

¼ teaspoon ground nutmeg

10 ounces ciabatta (from one 16- to 20-ounce loaf), cut into ¾- to 1-inch cubes (about 8 cups)

2 cups coarsely grated Gruyère (4 ounces)

1 cup finely grated Parmigiano-Reggiano cheese (2 ounces)

2¾ cups low-fat milk

9 large eggs

2 tablespoons Dijon mustard

Remove as much liquid from the thawed spinach as possible by squeezing it, then finely chop the spinach.

Melt the butter in a large, heavy skillet over medium-high heat; add the onion and sauté until soft, 4 to 5 minutes. Add ½ teaspoon of the salt, ¼ teaspoon of the pepper, and the nutmeg and cook, stirring, for 1 minute. Stir in the spinach and remove from the heat.

Spread half of the bread cubes in a 13 x 9 x 2-inch baking dish and top with half of the spinach mixture, spooning it over the bread evenly. Sprinkle with half of each cheese. Repeat the layers with the remaining bread, spinach mixture, and cheeses.

In a large bowl, whisk together the milk, eggs, mustard, and remaining ½ teaspoon of salt and ¼ teaspoon of pepper to blend. Pour the mixture evenly over the strata. Cover the strata with plastic wrap and refrigerate for at least 8 hours and up to 1 day.

Arrange the oven rack in the middle of the oven. Preheat the oven to 350°F. Let the strata stand at room temperature for 30 minutes.

Bake the strata, uncovered, until puffed, golden brown, and cooked through, 45 to 55 minutes. Let the strata stand for 5 minutes before serving.

WINE: Many white wines would work here, but a light-bodied Pinot Noir, such as Messina Hof's Private Reserve, Double Barrel Pinot Noir, is surprisingly responsive to the strata's savory character.

Southern Brunch Grits

Grits are a breakfast and brunch staple around the South, and for good reason. While I thought I held the secret to creamy grits by cooking them in a mixture of half-water, half-milk, it turns out I still had more to learn on the subject. Friend and fellow cookbook author Martha Hopkins, a Memphis native, taught me the wisdom in allowing grits to soak before cooking for even creamier results (without any milk). Speaking of creaminess, it's downright alarming how much cheese can go missing in a pot of grits undetected; for that reason, when I add cheese, I choose a sharp Cheddar that will stand out, and sprinkle it over the top. Skipping the cheese? A little nutritional yeast (a protein- and vitamin-rich seasoning available in natural foods markets) gives it a cheesy flavor boost. This is a good dish for pulling out the sriracha, too.

Makes 4 to 6 servings : : **Vegan Option • GF**

1 cup grits (not instant)

1 teaspoon kosher salt, plus more to taste

½ cup heavy whipping cream or (for vegan) Basic Cashew Cream (page 96)

1 cup loosely packed shredded sharp Cheddar cheese (2 to 3 ounces) or (for vegan) 2 teaspoons nutritional yeast

Freshly ground black pepper

Combine 5 cups of water, and the grits and salt in a medium, heavy saucepan, whisking to blend well. Cover and refrigerate for at least 1 hour and up to overnight.

Heat the covered grits mixture over medium-high heat, whisking occasionally, until the mixture comes to a simmer. Lower the heat to medium-low and simmer, covered, whisking occasionally, until the grits are cooked, bubbling, and thick, about 10 minutes. Whisk in the cream or cashew cream and return to a simmer. Remove from the heat. Whisk in the nutritional yeast now, if using. Season to taste with additional salt, if needed, and freshly ground black pepper. Transfer to a serving bowl and sprinkle with the grated cheese, if using. Serve warm.

Banana-Oat Pancakes
with Toasted Pecans

Pancakes get perked up with the addition of freshly ground oats and bananas, giving them added texture and sweetness in addition to making them more satisfying than standard fare. Cook them on a cast-iron griddle, if you have one. Top the pancakes with chopped toasted pecans, pure maple syrup, and additional fresh fruit, if you like.

Makes about fourteen 5-inch pancakes; 6 servings :: **Vegan Option**

2 cups old-fashioned rolled oats

1½ cups unbleached all-purpose flour

3 tablespoons organic granulated sugar

1 tablespoon baking powder

1 teaspoon cinnamon

½ teaspoon kosher salt

2½ cups 2% or whole organic milk or (for vegan) almond milk

3 large eggs or (for vegan) flax eggs (page 141)

¼ cup canola oil or melted coconut oil, plus more canola oil for griddle

2 small to medium-size bananas, chopped (about 1½ cups)

Additional fresh fruit, such as sliced bananas, peaches, or berries, for serving

Chopped toasted pecans, for serving

Pure maple syrup, for serving

Using a food processor, blend the oats until coarsely ground. Transfer the ground oats to a large mixing bowl. Add the flour, sugar, baking powder, cinnamon, and salt and whisk to blend well.

In a medium mixing bowl or large glass measuring cup, combine the milk or almond milk, and eggs or flax eggs, and whisk to blend well. Pour the wet ingredients over the dry ingredients and whisk to combine. Whisk in the ¼ cup oil. Fold in the bananas.

Brush the griddle with additional canola oil and heat over medium heat until the griddle is very hot.

Using a ladle, spoon batter onto the griddle, making large, 5-inch-diameter pancakes. Cook until bubbles form around the edges of the pancakes, then flip them and cook on the second side until done. Repeat with the remaining batter. Serve warm with additional fresh fruit, toasted pecans, and maple syrup.

Zucchini, Red Bell Pepper, and Gruyère Quiche

If you are close friends with my parents, Jeff and Susan Samuel, this is the quiche you might eat on Christmas morning. My mother has been known to bake half a dozen of the red-and-green-studded pies on Christmas Eve and make the rounds to friends' houses so they'll have something easy to warm in the oven the following day. That said, it's summertime when Texas gardens produce zucchini and peppers, so the recipe is just as useful in July. With quiche it's important to "blind bake" the crust—in other words, to bake it briefly before filling it—to avoid any underbaked pastry on the bottom.

Makes one 9-inch quiche; about 6 servings

Simple Pastry Crust (page 148)

3 teaspoons extra-virgin olive oil, divided

1 medium-size zucchini (5 to 6 ounces), sliced into ¼-inch-thick rounds

½ medium-size red bell pepper, seeded, sliced into ¼-inch-thick pieces

¾ cup half-and-half or heavy whipping cream

¾ cup whole milk

3 large eggs

¼ teaspoon kosher salt

¼ teaspoon freshly ground black or white pepper

1½ cups loosely packed grated Gruyère or aged Gouda cheese (about 4 ounces)

RECIPE CONTINUES

Preheat the oven to 450°F. Follow the Simple Pastry Crust recipe instructions for rolling out the dough and freezing the unbaked crust.

Remove the crust from the freezer, line it with parchment paper, and fill it with pie weights or dried beans. Bake the crust until the sides are set, 10 to 12 minutes.

Remove it from the oven, and remove the parchment paper lining and pie weights. Return the crust to the oven to bake the bottom of the crust just until it's dry in appearance, about 4 minutes longer. Remove from the oven; lower the heat to 350°F.

Heat 1½ teaspoons of the olive oil in a medium, heavy skillet over medium-high heat; add the zucchini and sauté until it's tender and just beginning to brown in spots, about 5 minutes. Season it to taste with salt; transfer the zucchini to a plate or bowl. Add the remaining 1½ teaspoons of olive oil to the same skillet and sauté the red bell pepper slices until they are just tender and beginning to brown in spots, about 5 minutes. Remove from the heat.

In a medium bowl, whisk the half-and-half, milk, and eggs to blend well. Whisk in ¼ teaspoon of salt and ¼ teaspoon of ground pepper.

Sprinkle the parbaked crust with the sautéed zucchini slices, then the peppers, fanning out from the center, if desired. Sprinkle the grated cheese evenly over the vegetables. Pour the egg mixture over the vegetables and cheese. Bake the quiche until it is puffed, the cheese on the top is turning golden, and it is just set in the center, about 45 minutes. Serve warm, at room temperature, or chilled.

Can be prepared up to 1 day ahead. Cover and refrigerate.

Simple Pastry Crust

I made piecrust in my food processor for years. It garnered such comments as, "Wow, it's not even flaky at all," from Till, my well-meaning husband, who'd apparently heard something about flakiness and piecrust but mixed up which sort was desirable. After a cooking class at Fort Worth's Central Market, I was converted to often doing this particular task the old-fashioned way to avoid the mistake of overworking the dough (which was the cause of my formerly unflaky crusts, sweetheart). Using very cold butter and as little water as possible helps too.

Makes one 9-inch piecrust

1½ cups unbleached all-purpose flour, plus more for rolling

½ teaspoon kosher salt

5 ounces (10 tablespoons) very cold unsalted butter

5 tablespoons ice water

In a medium bowl, whisk the flour and salt to blend.

Cut the cold butter into ½-inch pieces. Add the butter pieces to the flour mixture and gently rub the butter into the flour with your fingertips until the butter is incorporated (some large bits should remain).

Sprinkle the mixture with ice water, 1 tablespoon at a time, gently stirring with a fork until the dough just holds together. Knead briefly to pull the dough together. Flatten the dough into a disk, enclose it in plastic wrap, and refrigerate at least 30 minutes and up to 2 days.

Lay a large square of parchment paper on a work surface and sprinkle it lightly with flour. Place the chilled dough disk in the middle of the paper and sprinkle the dough lightly with flour (let it stand for 10 minutes if it's too stiff to roll). Roll the dough out into a 13-inch round. Transfer the dough to a 9-inch pie plate. Trim any excess overhang from the sides of the pie plate, and tuck the remaining overhang under, crimping the edges decoratively. Prick the bottom of the crust with a fork and freeze for 10 minutes before baking. (Save the parchment to line the crust for blind baking, and save any scraps for cutouts, if you like.)

MEATLESS IN COWTOWN

Best-Ever Banana Bread with Pecans and Chocolate Chips

Whenever bananas are overly ripe and going begging in our house, I make a loaf of this for a breakfast treat or an afternoon sweet. This recipe is a riff on one from my great-great-aunt Tee, who, of course, made hers with Crisco. I've taken several liberties with her recipe, discovering that using coconut oil really takes it to the next level. And instead of stirring the nuts into the batter, I sprinkle them on top, where they can crisp up nicely (just don't use too many or it can weigh the bread down). Aunt Tee was never known to add chocolate chips to the mix, either, but while we're improving upon tradition, why not?

Makes one 8½ x 4½ x 3-inch loaf :: **Vegan Option**

1¾ cups organic all-purpose flour

2 teaspoons baking powder

¾ teaspoon salt

¼ teaspoon baking soda

2 medium-size overripe bananas (it's best if they have brown speckles on them), mashed (about 1 cup)

½ cup 2% or whole milk or (for vegan) almond milk

1 teaspoon vanilla extract

1 cup organic granulated sugar

¼ cup plus 2 tablespoons coconut oil, melted

2 large eggs or (for vegan) flax eggs (page 141)

1 cup (scant) semisweet mini chocolate chips or bittersweet chocolate chips (vegan, if desired; optional)

½ cup (scant) pecan halves or walnut pieces, chopped

Preheat the oven to 350°F. Oil an 8½ x 4½ x 3-inch loaf pan or line it with parchment paper.

In a medium mixing bowl, whisk the flour, baking powder, salt, and baking soda to blend and set aside.

In a small mixing bowl, stir the mashed bananas, milk or almond milk, and vanilla to combine and set aside.

Using an electric mixer on medium speed, beat the sugar and coconut oil in a large bowl to blend. Add the eggs one at a time or flax eggs all together, beating well. Beat the flour and banana mixtures into the sugar mixture alternately, in two additions each. Fold in the chocolate chips, if using. Pour the batter into the prepared pan, sprinkle the top evenly with the nuts, and bake until the bread is puffed, golden, and a tester inserted into the center comes out with moist crumbs attached, 45 to 55 minutes.

Can be prepared up to 1 week ahead. Let cool, then seal in an airtight container and freeze. Thaw at room temperature.

Spiced Applesauce Muffins
with Walnut-Oat Streusel

These muffins come together quickly with such pantry staples as unsweetened applesauce and warm autumnal spices (improvise if you don't have them all—the spice mixture sold as "pumpkin pie spice" is fine). A generous cap of streusel topping adds crunch and heft. Enjoy with a cup of tea or coffee.

Makes 12 muffins :: **Vegan Option**

Muffins

1 cup unbleached all-purpose flour

½ cup white whole wheat flour

2 teaspoons baking powder

½ teaspoon ground cinnamon

¼ teaspoon ground ginger

¼ teaspoon ground allspice

⅛ teaspoon ground cloves

¼ teaspoon kosher salt

2 large eggs or (for vegan) flax eggs (page 141)

1 cup organic granulated sugar

1 cup unsweetened applesauce

½ cup melted coconut oil or canola oil

Streusel

1 cup walnut halves, coarsely chopped

½ cup old-fashioned rolled oats

3 tablespoons organic granulated sugar

3 tablespoons chilled unsalted butter or vegan butter stick (such as Earth Balance), cubed

To make the muffins: Preheat the oven to 400°F. Line a standard-size muffin tin with parchment paper baking cups.

In a medium bowl, whisk both flours, the baking powder, all the spices, and the salt to combine well. In a large bowl, whisk the eggs or flax eggs to blend. Add the sugar and whisk well. Whisk in the applesauce, then the oil. Add the flour mixture to the applesauce mixture and whisk to blend well (the batter will be thick). Spoon the batter equally among the prepared muffin cups.

To make the streusel: In a small bowl, combine the walnuts, oats, and sugar, tossing to mix. Add the butter or vegan butter, working it into the dry mixture with your fingertips to form clumps of streusel. Sprinkle the streusel evenly over the unbaked muffins.

Bake the muffins until puffed and set in the center, 20 to 22 minutes. Let cool at least 5 minutes. Serve warm or at room temperature.

BEER: Serving these muffins for dessert? The crisp-tart nature of Jester King's Ambrée Farmhouse Amber Ale elevates them with its own fruit cocktail of flavors and baked bread notes.

Migas with Peppers and Onions

This scrambled-egg-with-corn-tortillas oddity is something I'd never heard of when I moved to Texas; now, seeing it on breakfast and brunch menus always makes me feel at home. It also makes for a great weekend brunch dish, or an easy-to-throw-together dinner.

Serves 4 :: **GF**

4 tablespoons canola or light olive oil, divided

5 corn tortillas (gluten-free, if desired)

6 large eggs

⅓ cup whole milk

¼ teaspoon kosher salt

¼ teaspoon freshly ground black pepper

½ medium-size yellow onion, chopped (about 1 cup)

1 large poblano chile, stemmed, seeded, and minced (about ¾ cup)

1 large jalapeño pepper, seeded and minced (about ¼ cup)

6 ounces fresh tomatoes (about 2 large Roma tomatoes), seeded and finely chopped (1 scant cup)

Line a large plate with paper towels. Heat 3 tablespoons of the oil in a small, heavy skillet over medium-high heat. Add one tortilla at a time and fry until puffed and beginning to brown in spots, turning once, about 1 minute total. Transfer the fried tortilla to the paper towel–lined plate to drain. Repeat with the remaining tortillas. Stack the fried tortillas on a cutting board and chop into 1-inch pieces. Set aside.

In a medium bowl, whisk the eggs, milk, salt, and pepper to blend.

Heat the remaining 1 tablespoon oil in a large, heavy nonstick skillet over medium-high heat. Add the onion and sauté until tender and translucent, about 3 minutes. Add the poblano and jalapeño and sauté until just beginning to soften, about 2 minutes. Add the tomatoes and sauté until the tomatoes just begin to soften, about 2 minutes. Add the tortilla pieces and sauté until heated through, about 1 minute. Add the egg mixture and stir until the eggs are scrambled and cooked through, about 5 minutes. Serve warm.

Coconut-Scented Pumpkin Bread with Pepitas

What happens when you take the four eggs out of the classic pumpkin bread recipe? Amazingly, nothing is lost—except perhaps a bit of height. This recipe gets its luscious coconuttiness from coconut milk, coconut oil, and a sprinkling of coconut on top. Together with raw pepitas, the toppings toast to the perfect level of crunchiness as these loaves bake.

Makes two 8½ x 4½ x 3-inch loaves :: **V**

2 cups unbleached all-purpose flour

1½ cups white whole wheat flour

2 teaspoons baking soda

1 teaspoon kosher salt

1 teaspoon ground cinnamon

½ teaspoon baking powder

¼ teaspoon ground nutmeg

⅛ teaspoon ground cloves (optional)

1½ cups organic granulated sugar

1 cup (packed) organic light or dark brown sugar

1 (15-ounce) can pure pumpkin purée

⅔ cup coconut milk (from 1 [13.5-ounce] can)

½ cup canola oil or light-flavored olive oil

⅓ cup melted coconut oil

2 tablespoons raw pepitas

2 tablespoons sweetened shredded coconut

Preheat the oven to 350°F. Oil two 8½ x 4½ x 3-inch loaf pans, or line them with parchment paper.

In a medium bowl, combine both flours and the baking soda, salt, cinnamon, baking powder, nutmeg, and cloves, if using; whisk to blend well. In a large bowl, combine the granulated sugar, brown sugar, pumpkin, coconut milk, and both oils; using an electric mixer, beat on medium speed to blend well.

Add the dry ingredients to the pumpkin mixture and beat just until incorporated. (The batter will be fairly thick.)

Divide the batter between the prepared pans. Sprinkle each loaf evenly with 1 tablespoon of pepitas and 1 tablespoon of shredded coconut. Bake the pumpkin bread until it springs back lightly to the touch on the sides, and a tester inserted into the center comes out clean, 50 to 55 minutes. Serve warm or at room temperature.

Pumpkin bread freezes well. Slice, seal in airtight container, and freeze; reheat or thaw at room temperature before serving.

Potato, Onion, and Egg Torta

It's hard to improve on the classic Torta Espanola, the perfect main dish for brunch, lunch, or dinner. Only a few ingredients and a half-hour of cooking—it's even kid-friendly. Serve it plain or garnish it with a dollop of guacamole or sour cream, or a few crumbles of queso fresco and some snipped chives.

Serves 6 :: **GF**

1½ to 1¾ pounds Yukon gold potatoes (about 5 medium-size), peeled

1 medium sweet onion (about 12 ounces), peeled

½ cup olive oil

7 large eggs

¾ teaspoon kosher salt

¼ teaspoon freshly ground black pepper

Using a food processor fitted with its thinnest slicing blade or using a mandoline, thinly slice the potatoes and onions.

Heat the oil in a 12-inch heavy nonstick skillet over medium-high heat. Add the sliced potatoes and onion and cook, stirring frequently so that the oil gets between the potato and onion slices, until the onion is translucent and soft and the potatoes are soft in the middle, 15 to 18 minutes.

Set a metal colander over a large bowl and drain the potato mixture while preparing the eggs (reserve the oil that collects in the bowl; you will need at least 2 tablespoons of it).

Whisk the eggs, salt, and pepper in a very large bowl to blend. Add the potato mixture and fold to combine.

Return the nonstick skillet to medium-high heat, adding 1 tablespoon of the oil reserved from cooking the potato mixture. When the oil is hot, add the egg mixture to the skillet. Cook, shaking gently and running a rubber spatula around the sides to loosen from the pan, until the edges and bottom are golden brown and the eggs are set around the edge and underneath (the top will be very runny), 5 to 8 minutes.

Using oven mitts, hold a heatproof platter atop the skillet and flip it over, so the torta is transferred to the plate cooked-side up. Add another tablespoon of the reserved oil to the hot skillet and slide the torta back into the skillet. Cook the torta until golden brown on the bottom (do not overcook), about 5 minutes longer. Loosen the torta from the sides of the pan with a rubber spatula and slide it out onto a clean platter. Let stand for 10 minutes before serving. Slice into wedges and serve.

SWEET ONIONS

Georgia has its Vidalias and Hawaii has its Mauis, but Texas has its own supersweet onions: Texas 1015s. Developed by Texas A&M and named for October 15, their ideal planting date, these pale yellow-skinned beauties have a very sweet, mild, white flesh. They're grown in South Texas's Rio Grande Valley, best known for its citrus, and they hit markets in the spring. In North Texas, we have another region-specific sweet onion, Noondays, grown exclusively within a 10-mile radius of the small town of Noonday, just south of Tyler. (When grown outside of Noonday, these onions are known as Yellow Granex, the same variety used for Vidalias and Mauis.) Sweet onions are ideal for using raw in salsas and salad, but they're also divine grilled (such as in fajitas; see page 99), stewed (try the ratatouille, page 94), and featured in the Potato, Onion, and Egg Torta (page 154).

SIDE DISHES

ROASTED CAULIFLOWER AND GARLIC 158

MAPLE- AND CUMIN-ROASTED CARROTS
AND PARSNIPS 160

CILANTRO-LIME TEXAS BASMATI 161

GRILLED LEMON-DIJON
BRUSSELS SPROUTS 163

ROSEMARY YUKON GOLD
SMASHED POTATOES 164

GINGERED CABBAGE AND JICAMA SLAW
WITH SNOW PEAS 165

ACCORDION-STYLE SWEET POTATOES
WITH CHILI SALT AND GARLIC 166

MEXICAN-STYLE CORN ON THE COB
WITH CILANTRO-CHILI AÏOLI 168

CILANTRO-CHILI AÏOLI 169

BARBECUE BAKED BEANS 171

STEAKHOUSE-STYLE CREAMED SPINACH 172

HOMEMADE CORN TORTILLAS 173

For the meatless in Cowtown, whether at home, at a party, or at a restaurant, side dishes often become the main course. But that doesn't mean it won't be a satisfying meal. Need convincing? Try the Accordion-Style Sweet Potatoes with Chili Salt and Garlic served alongside the Baby Greens Salad with Avocado and Creamy Tahini-Ginger Vinaigrette, or the Cilantro-Lime Texas Basmati topped with Black Beans Simmered with Onion and Jalapeño. The sides-as-main approach is especially handy for navigating restaurants that don't—at first glance—seem to have any meatless options on the menu. Scan through the meat dishes to see which sides they're served with and you should be able to sweet-talk your way into a unique veggie plate that's better than anything else on the menu.

Roasted Cauliflower and Garlic

Sweet and smoky, roasted cauliflower turns the otherwise bland vegetable into a side dish you'll find surprisingly addictive. Let the cauliflower get a little browned on the edges, and make this easy side dish with or without the whole garlic cloves. If you do include them, you'll be rewarded with garlic that's sweet enough to eat whole and soft enough to spread on bread. For a spicy version, whisk the oil with ¼ teaspoon each of cayenne, coriander, cumin, ginger, and turmeric.

Makes 4 to 6 side-dish servings :: **V • GF**

1 large head (at least 2 pounds) cauliflower, separated into florets

1 head of garlic, cloves separated and peeled

¼ cup extra-virgin olive oil

1 teaspoon kosher salt

Preheat the oven to 425°F. Line a large baking dish with parchment paper. Place the cauliflower florets and garlic cloves in a large bowl. Pour the oil over the cauliflower and garlic and toss to coat. Sprinkle with the salt and toss to coat again.

Transfer to the prepared roasting pan (the cauliflower should be in a tight single layer—not too spread out or the garlic could burn). Roast, stirring occasionally, until the cauliflower is cooked through and beginning to brown in spots and the garlic is tender, 25 to 30 minutes. Serve warm or at room temperature.

Maple- and Cumin-Roasted Carrots and Parsnips

Carrots were one of our first gardening successes in Texas, which helped ease the pain of realizing that large slicing tomatoes would not come easily—if at all—in these parts. Carrots grow so well in Texas, in fact, that they're a big commercial crop. Parsnips have a delicate but distinctive flavor and are very sweet when roasted. If you're not a fan of parsnips, this recipe also works well with 2 pounds of carrots.

Makes 4 to 6 side-dish servings :: **V • GF**

1 pound carrots, trimmed and peeled

1 pound parsnips, trimmed and peeled

3 tablespoons extra-virgin olive oil

1 tablespoon pure maple syrup

½ teaspoon kosher salt

½ teaspoon ground cumin

Fresh herbs, such as fresh flat-leaf parsley leaves or snipped chives for garnish (optional)

Preheat the oven to 400°F. Line two 13 x 9 x 2-inch baking dishes with parchment paper.

Cut the carrots and parsnips into uniform sticks about 3 inches long and ½ inch thick. Transfer the vegetables to a large bowl.

In a small bowl, whisk the olive oil, maple syrup, salt, and cumin to blend. Drizzle over the vegetables, tossing to coat, and divide evenly between the prepared dishes, spreading out in a single layer. Roast the vegetables, stirring occasionally, until the carrots and parsnips are tender all the way through and beginning to brown in spots, 40 to 45 minutes. Serve warm or at room temperature, garnishing with fresh herbs, if desired.

Cilantro-Lime Texas Basmati

When there's brown rice and water bubbling in the rice cooker or on the stove, I feel like dinner is underway—even if I haven't determined exactly what else it will include just yet. I often use Rice Select's Organic Texmati Brown Rice, which is a basmati-style rice grown in southeast Texas; I also like Trader Joe's brown basmati, which has a light, fluffy texture. While I often prepare brown rice simply with water, a glug of olive oil, and pinch of salt, if you have an extra five minutes, it's fun to make things a little more interesting. Cilantro-Lime Texas Basmati makes a delicious bed for a ladleful of the Black Beans Simmered with Onion and Jalapeño (page 118); the flavors complement each other and together make a simple, satisfying meal that's vegan and gluten-free, too.

Makes about 4 cups rice; doubles easily :: **V • GF**

1 cup brown basmati rice

¼ teaspoon kosher salt, plus more to taste

½ teaspoon plus 2 tablespoons extra-virgin olive oil, divided

2 tablespoons freshly squeezed lime juice

½ cup loosely packed fresh cilantro leaves, coarsely chopped

Place 2 cups of water, the rice, ¼ teaspoon of the salt, and ½ teaspoon of the olive oil in a medium, heavy pot or a rice cooker, stirring to combine. If cooking on the stovetop, cover the pot and bring to a boil, then lower the heat to low and simmer until the rice is fully cooked, about 40 minutes. (If using a rice cooker, simply cover the insert with the lid and turn it on.)

Meanwhile, in a small bowl, whisk the remaining 2 tablespoons of olive oil and the lime juice and cilantro to combine (alternatively, blend the cilantro into the remaining oil and lime juice in the blender).

Transfer the cooked rice to a serving bowl, fluffing with a fork. Drizzle the cilantro mixture over the rice, toss to coat, and season to taste with additional salt, if desired. Serve warm.

Grilled Lemon-Dijon Brussels Sprouts

There are two kinds of people: those who love Brussels sprouts and those who would love Brussels sprouts if they would prepare them with a lighter hand. Crisp-tender, the sprouts are delectable; overcooked, they are barely passable. If you can find a large stalk of fresh Brussels sprouts, which show up in markets in the late fall, it's just what you need for this recipe. The grill gives these a wonderful smokiness, but roasting works, too.

Makes 6 to 8 servings :: **V • GF**

2 pounds fresh Brussels sprouts, washed and trimmed

¼ cup extra-virgin olive oil

2 tablespoons freshly squeezed lemon juice

1 tablespoon Dijon mustard

¼ teaspoon kosher salt

Place a perforated stainless-steel grill topper on the grill (see sidebar, page 105). Preheat the grill to medium-high heat (about 375°F).

Halve the Brussels sprouts vertically through the stem and place them in a large bowl (if they are very small, just leave them whole).

In a small bowl, whisk the olive oil, lemon juice, mustard, and salt to blend. Pour half of the olive oil mixture over the Brussels sprouts; using your hands, toss to coat. Add enough of the remaining olive oil mixture to coat the Brussels sprouts (you will need most, if not all of it).

Pour the dressed Brussels sprouts onto the preheated grill pan. Close the grill cover and grill the sprouts, stirring every 3 to 4 minutes, until the sprouts are bright green and beginning to char in spots, 10 to 12 minutes total.

Alternatively, to roast the sprouts, preheat the oven to 450°F. Line two large baking dishes with parchment paper, and divide the dressed Brussels sprouts between the dishes. Roast, stirring occasionally, until the Brussels sprouts are crisp-tender and beginning to brown in spots, 20 to 25 minutes.

Serve warm or at room temperature.

Rosemary Yukon Gold Smashed Potatoes

Yukon Gold potatoes are great in this recipe because of their buttery texture and taste. You can use any size potatoes, but the boiling time will vary, so choose ones that are relatively uniform in size. We had these at our Hays County Thanksgiving while working on this book together—and they were a hit.

Makes 8 to 10 servings :: **V • GF**

2 pounds Yukon gold potatoes, scrubbed, skin left on

½ cup extra-virgin olive oil

1 tablespoon chopped fresh rosemary

1½ teaspoons kosher salt, divided

Line a rimmed baking sheet or a large roasting pan with parchment paper.

Fill a large pot three-quarters full with salted water. Add the whole potatoes to the cold water, cover, and bring to a boil over medium-high heat. Lower the heat to low and simmer until the potatoes are tender (a knife inserted should slide in easily), about 25 minutes (the boiling time will vary depending on the size of potatoes). Remove from the heat; drain the potatoes in a colander.

Preheat the oven to 450°F. Whisk the olive oil, rosemary, and 1 teaspoon of the salt in a small bowl to blend. Using a pastry brush, brush one side of each potato and place them oiled-side down in the prepared pan. Using the back of a large wooden or metal spoon, slowly but firmly press down on each potato until it smashes down to a 1- to 1½-inch thickness. Brush the tops and sides of the potatoes liberally with the remaining olive oil mixture. Sprinkle the potatoes with the remaining ½ teaspoon of kosher salt. Bake until the potatoes are just beginning to brown on top and the edges look crisp, 30 to 35 minutes.

Gingered Cabbage and Jicama Slaw with Snow Peas

A food processor with a shredding blade makes this colorful slaw come together quickly.

Makes about 10 servings :: **Vegan Option • GF**

½ medium-size head green cabbage (from a 2½-pound cabbage), cored

½ medium-size jicama (from a 1-pound jicama), peeled

2 large carrots (about 7 ounces), peeled

1 medium-size red bell pepper (about 6 ounces), stemmed, seeded, and cut into matchstick-size strips

8 ounces snow peas, stringed

½ cup mayonnaise or vegan mayonnaise (such as Vegenaise)

2 tablespoons freshly squeezed lemon juice

2 tablespoons agave nectar

1 tablespoon peeled and minced fresh ginger

¼ teaspoon kosher salt, or more to taste

⅛ teaspoon freshly ground black pepper, or more to taste

Fit a food processor with the shredding blade. Shred the cabbage, jicama, and carrots. Transfer the shredded vegetables to a large bowl. Add the red bell pepper strips to the vegetable mixture.

Fit a steamer insert into a pot and fill with 1 to 2 inches of water (the water should not touch the bottom of the steam insert). Bring the water to a boil, add the snow peas, cover, and steam until the snow peas are bright green in color and crisp-tender, 1 to 2 minutes.

Rinse the snow peas under cold water to stop the cooking. Drain and place them on a cutting board; cut them diagonally into thirds, then add to the vegetable mixture.

In a small bowl, whisk the mayonnaise or vegan mayonnaise, lemon juice, agave nectar, ginger, salt, and pepper to blend. Pour the dressing over the shredded vegetables and toss to coat. Season to taste with additional salt and pepper, if desired. Cover and chill for at least 1 hour and up to 1 day. Serve cold.

Accordion-Style Sweet Potatoes with Chili Salt and Garlic

This style of preparing potatoes is popular for good reason: Not only are they visually striking, you also get some of the benefits of a gratin—thin, tender slices and deliciously crusty edges—without the heavy sauce. I especially like this technique for sweet potatoes, which are grown in Texas much of the year.

Makes about 4 servings :: **V • GF**

4 small to medium-size sweet potatoes (2 to 2¼ pounds), peeled

4 large garlic cloves, peeled and very thinly sliced

¼ cup extra-virgin olive oil

1 teaspoon chili powder

¾ teaspoon kosher salt

Preheat the oven to 425°F. Line a large baking dish with parchment paper.

Place the peeled sweet potatoes on a work surface. Using two wooden spoon handles as a guide along both long sides of one potato (to prevent the knife from slicing all the way through the potato), slice the potato crosswise into very thin slices that go at least three quarters of the way through. Gently slide one very thin garlic slice between every other slice in the sweet potato (the garlic slices will help to hold the sweet potato slices slightly apart). Repeat with the remaining potatoes and garlic slices.

In a small bowl, whisk the oil, chili powder, and salt to blend. Using a pastry brush, generously brush the mixture all over the potatoes. Place the potatoes in the prepared dish. Brush the mixture again over the tops of the potatoes a couple of times, allowing the oil to drip between the slices (some of the oil mixture might be left over).

Bake until the sweet potatoes are tender all the way through and the tops of the slices are beginning to get crusty and golden brown, 1 hour 10 minutes to 1 hour 15 minutes. Serve warm or at room temperature.

Mexican-Style Corn on the Cob with Cilantro-Chili Aïoli

I love summer food, and this classic dish is a great example of why. Fresh corn on the cob gets grilled and then slathered in a rich sauce for an irresistible side dish. While this recipe is best prepared with grilled corn, it's also worth preparing with boiled corn if grilling isn't in your plans; find instructions for either below.

Makes 6 servings :: **Vegan Option • GF**

6 ears fresh corn, shucked and rinsed (remove as much of the corn silk as possible)

1 tablespoon canola or olive oil

Cilantro-Chili Aïoli (page 169)

2 ounces cotija cheese, crumbled (about ½ cup), for serving (optional; omit for vegan)

½ lime, cut into 6 wedges, for serving

To grill the corn: Preheat the grill to 425°F. Brush the shucked corn with oil. Grill the corn, turning every 3 minutes, until the kernels are tender and just beginning to brown in a few spots, about 9 minutes total. Transfer the corn to a serving platter.

To boil the corn instead: Bring a large pot of salted water to a boil. Drop in the husked corn, cover, and cook 5 minutes. Drain in a colander, and rinse with cold water to stop the cooking. Transfer the corn to a serving platter.

Spread the aïoli over the warm cooked corn on the platter, turning it to cover all sides. Sprinkle the corn generously with the crumbled cotija, if using. Place lime wedges on the platter. Serve the corn warm with the lime wedges to squeeze over it.

MEATLESS IN COWTOWN

Cilantro-Chili Aïoli

This is a natural on grilled corn, but it also makes a flavorful dipping sauce for green vegetables, such as okra or asparagus.

Makes about ½ cup aïoli :: **Vegan Option • GF**

½ cup mayonnaise or vegan mayonnaise (such as Vegenaise)

¼ cup loosely packed fresh cilantro leaves, chopped

1 garlic clove, peeled and minced

½ teaspoon chili powder

⅛ teaspoon chipotle chili powder

In a small bowl, whisk mayonnaise or vegan mayonnaise, cilantro, garlic, and both chili powders to blend. Can be prepared up to 2 days ahead of time. Cover and refrigerate until ready to serve.

Barbecue Baked Beans

The traditional side dish is usually weighed down with bacon, but nobody will miss it in this spicy version. Serve these with slaw and something from the grill.

Makes about 6 servings :: **V**

2 tablespoons extra-virgin olive oil

1 small (or ½ medium-size) white onion, chopped (about 1 cup)

1 cup Sweet and Spicy Barbecue Sauce (page 123)

2 tablespoons whiskey (such as Balcones True Blue Corn Whisky)

3 (15-ounce) cans pinto beans, drained and rinsed, or 4½ cups Garlicky Pinto Beans (page 76)

Preheat the oven to 350°F. Heat the olive oil in a large, heavy skillet over medium-high heat. Add the onion and sauté until tender and translucent, about 5 minutes. Stir in the barbecue sauce, ½ cup of water, and the whiskey and bring to a simmer. Stir in the beans to coat with sauce.

Transfer the beans to an 8-inch square baking dish. Cover with foil and bake until the sauce bubbles and thickens, about 50 minutes (uncover for the last 15 minutes of baking if you like a crusty top). Serve warm.

Steakhouse-Style Creamed Spinach

My version of creamed spinach calls for a whole pound of fresh baby spinach leaves. It's sold in a 1-pound clear plastic container at many markets, and it looks like too much at first, but it cooks down dramatically. This is wonderful as a side dish or as a baked potato topping (see instructions for perfectly baked potatoes below). Have picky eaters at the table? An immersion blender purées this into a silky green sauce that children love.

Makes about 6 servings :: **Gluten-Free Option**

2 tablespoons unsalted butter

1 large or 2 small shallots, peeled and minced (about ¼ cup)

2 tablespoons unbleached all-purpose flour or (for gluten-free) cornstarch

1½ cups whole milk

¼ teaspoon kosher salt, plus more to taste

⅛ teaspoon ground nutmeg

1 pound fresh baby spinach leaves

¼ cup shredded or grated Parmesan cheese (optional)

Freshly ground pepper

In a medium, heavy saucepan, melt the butter over medium-high heat. Add the shallot and sauté until tender and translucent, about 2 minutes. Sprinkle the flour or cornstarch over the shallot and stir with a wooden spoon; let the roux bubble and cook for 1 to 2 minutes longer (do not allow it to brown).

Add the milk and whisk until the sauce is bubbling and thickened, about 3 minutes. Lower the heat to medium. Whisk in the salt and nutmeg. Add as many spinach leaves as will fit in the pot and stir just until they've wilted, about 1 minute. Repeat, adding the remaining spinach leaves and stirring just until they've wilted and the mixture is bubbling and heated through (do not overcook).

Remove from the heat. Stir in the Parmesan cheese, if desired, and season to taste with salt and pepper. Serve warm.

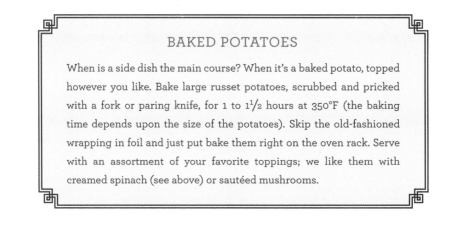

BAKED POTATOES

When is a side dish the main course? When it's a baked potato, topped however you like. Bake large russet potatoes, scrubbed and pricked with a fork or paring knife, for 1 to 1½ hours at 350°F (the baking time depends upon the size of the potatoes). Skip the old-fashioned wrapping in foil and just put bake them right on the oven rack. Serve with an assortment of your favorite toppings; we like them with creamed spinach (see above) or sautéed mushrooms.

Homemade Corn Tortillas

They take a little bit of practice (see page 175 for tips), but once you get the hang of making homemade tortillas, there's nothing simpler. Serve warm—preferably within an hour or so of making them—with fajitas (see page 99), soft tacos (see page 117), or as a side dish with any meal that includes beans and rice.

Makes twelve 6-inch tortillas :: **V • GF**

2 cups masa harina

1 teaspoon kosher salt

3 tablespoons canola oil or extra-virgin olive oil, plus
    more for canola griddle, if needed

1½ cups warm water

Place the masa harina in a large bowl. Using a fork, stir in the salt, then the oil. Stir in 1¼ to 1½ cups warm water until a soft dough forms. Using your hands, knead the dough a bit until it comes together and is uniform in texture (it will be soft and a bit sticky, the texture of Play-Doh). Cover the dough with plastic wrap and let it stand at room temperature for 30 minutes.

Preheat a cast-iron griddle over medium-high heat until very hot, brushing with oil if needed; lower the heat to medium. Line a large plate with a clean dish towel (choose a towel that's not at all fuzzy, such as a tea towel; this is for keeping the tortillas warm), or place a tortilla warmer near the stove.

Line a tortilla press with a double thickness of parchment paper. Divide the dough into twelve equal pieces; roll each piece of dough into a ball. Place one dough ball between the two sheets of parchment paper in the center of the tortilla press, and close firmly. Rotate the parchment and dough 90 degrees and close the press firmly again.

Transfer the tortilla to the preheated griddle and cook until dry, turning once, about 2 minutes total. Transfer the warm tortilla to the dish towel–lined plate, folding the towel over to enclose the tortilla, or to the tortilla warmer. Repeat with the remaining dough and tortillas. The tortillas will steam in the dish towel or tortilla warmer, softening as they stand. Serve warm.

TURNING OUT TORTILLAS

They require so few ingredients and so few steps, but mastering tortillas from scratch still takes a bit of practice. My first mistake was buying a cheap aluminum tortilla press; if you look at it from the side, you can see that the plates aren't flush, so the fact that it turns out thicker-than-desired tortillas should not be surprising. Next, I bought a plastic one from a Mexican foods market. I broke it with the very first press, snapping off the handle as I pushed down. (Maybe I was a little too excited about those tortillas.) In spite of my track record, a Fort Worth neighbor let me borrow her cast-iron one, and finally, fresh corn tortillas were mine. I've since purchased my own cast-iron press, choosing an 8-inch-diameter version so I can make small or medium-size tortillas. Other things to keep in mind include allowing the dough to rest long enough to rehydrate the masa (about 30 minutes) and skipping the recipe on the masa package, which, in my experience, produces too-dry results (instead, follow the recipe on page 173). Many tortilla makers swear by cooking on cast iron, so this is another time I pull out my favorite griddle. It covers two burners and can cook up to three tortillas at a time. While I used to think that tortilla warmers were just for keeping tortillas warm, it turns out that enclosing the freshly made tortillas steams them as they sit. A similar result can be achieved by enclosing them in a clean dish towel immediately after they're cooked. This is a critical step in preparing them, as it softens the tortillas and makes them more pliable than when they first come off the griddle.

DESSERTS

When I became vegetarian at the tender age of sixteen, I was confused as to why some people made the presumption that someone who doesn't eat meat would be any less interested in desserts. Back then, when airlines still served full meals, the vegetarian tray might come with a fig bar, while the regular meal was more likely to have a fudge brownie. (My sister found this to be funny; I thought it was frustrating.) Later, as a food magazine editor, I took a series of professional baking classes to develop my area of interest into a specialty of sorts. Over the years, my longtime love of sweets and baking has gradually shifted toward more wholesome ingredients. In addition to buying organic, and folding some whole grains into the mix where possible, I've also tested some of my favorite desserts with vegan ingredients. From All-Natural Red Velvet Bundt Cake to Nutty Oatmeal Cookies with Dried Fruit, desserts are for everyone.

Texas Peach Cobbler

My mother-in-law, Virginia Meyn, excels at fresh fruit desserts. She gave me her version of this cobbler, which she'd adapted from a recipe written by her grandmother, Mama Cox. Traditional cobblers often have a thicker, more biscuitlike topping; this delicious one is perhaps closer to a French clafouti. Mama Cox, who lived in a farmhouse in Bluff City, Tennessee, made her cobbler with two cups of fresh blackberries, which are ripe late spring in Texas. I love it with sliced peaches, which are fresh all summer in North Texas (the Parker County Peach festival is held every July in Weatherford). I've adapted it to swap out the butter for coconut oil, and also added a splash of amaretto to the fruit. Try it any which way, but do try it: It's an incredibly forgiving recipe, as its many successful versions prove.

Makes about 8 servings

2½ pounds fresh ripe peaches (about 5 large)

1 tablespoon amaretto

2 tablespoons plus 1 cup organic granulated sugar, divided

1 tablespoon cornstarch

1 teaspoon ground cinnamon

1 cup unbleached all-purpose flour

2 teaspoons baking powder

1 teaspoon (scant) kosher salt

1 cup whole milk

1 large egg

1 teaspoon vanilla extract

3 tablespoons melted coconut oil or unsalted butter

Ice cream, for serving (optional)

Preheat the oven to 375°F.

Pit, peel, and slice the peaches into ½- to ¾-inch-thick slices; place them in a large bowl. Sprinkle the peaches with the amaretto and toss to combine. Add 2 tablespoons of the sugar and the cornstarch and cinnamon and toss to coat.

In a large bowl, whisk the flour, remaining 1 cup of sugar, baking powder, and salt to blend. In a medium bowl, whisk the milk, egg, and vanilla to blend. Add the milk mixture to the flour mixture and whisk to blend, making a thin batter.

Pour the coconut oil into a 13 x 9 x 2-inch glass or ceramic baking dish, tilting the dish to evenly coat the bottom. Pour the batter atop the oil, and top the batter with the fruit mixture. Bake until the fruit is tender and the batter is baked through, puffed, and golden around the edges, 40 to 45 minutes. Serve warm with ice cream, if desired.

Chocolate Chip–Whole Wheat Brownies

Brownies are already so dense that the use of whole wheat flour—especially the lighter-textured white whole wheat—is barely detectable, and making this simple switch more than triples the fiber. My family likes these studded with dark chocolate chips, but feel free to adapt it to your tastes. I always bake these in my Baker's Edge pan; it might look like a gimmick, but this serpentine pan really turns out evenly baked brownies. Enjoy these as a teatime treat; for dinner parties, serve them with ice cream and Warm Chocolate-Whiskey Sauce (see page 180).

Makes about 16

4 tablespoons (½ stick) unsalted butter

¼ cup canola oil or melted coconut oil

1 cup semisweet chocolate chips

1 cup organic granulated sugar

3 large eggs

1 teaspoon vanilla extract

½ teaspoon kosher salt

1¼ cups white whole wheat flour (regular whole wheat, unbleached all-purpose, or a combination of the two also will work)

1 cup bittersweet chocolate chips

Preheat the oven to 350°F. Line an 8-inch square baking dish with parchment paper or oil a Baker's Edge pan.

In a medium, heavy saucepan, heat the butter and oil together over low heat just until the butter melts; remove from the heat.

Add the semisweet chocolate chips and whisk until melted and smooth. Whisk in the sugar, then add the eggs one at a time, whisking briskly after each addition. Add the vanilla and salt and whisk to blend well. Add the flour and whisk until blended. Fold in the bittersweet chocolate chips.

Transfer the batter to the prepared pan and bake until puffed and set but soft in the center, 18 to 20 minutes. Serve warm or at room temperature. (Can be made ahead; store airtight at room temperature or freeze.)

Warm Chocolate-Whiskey Sauce

Drizzle it over traditional or coconut milk ice cream. This simple chocolate sauce is thick, rich, and can be spiked for the grown-ups.

Makes about 1 cup sauce :: **V • Gluten-Free Option**

½ cup light or full-fat coconut milk (from a 14-ounce can)

¼ cup agave nectar

1 cup chopped bittersweet chocolate (5 to 6 ounces; vegan, if desired)

1 to 2 tablespoons whiskey or bourbon (optional; omit for gluten-free)

Heat the coconut milk and agave nectar in a small, heavy saucepan over medium heat, whisking to combine. Bring to a simmer, add the chocolate, and remove from the heat. Let stand for 1 minute. Whisk the mixture until the chocolate is melted and smooth. Whisk in 1 tablespoon of the whiskey, if desired, adding more to taste. Serve warm. Can be prepared ahead. Let cool, then cover and refrigerate. Reheat over low heat.

Giant Chocolate Chip–Oatmeal Cookies with Walnuts

Like everyone else, I started out in life baking chocolate chip cookies with the Toll House recipe. But I fell for a man who knows his way around the kitchen, and I was astounded to find that he baked better chocolate chip cookies than I did (back then, anyway). His secret? Adding a generous helping of rolled oats to the classic recipe. Over the years, our recipe has undergone significant changes, and our cookies now are the best they've ever been. I love it that these are decadent as cookies should be, but that they're more satisfying because they're loaded with whole grains and nuts and have enough heft to actually hold you over till dinnertime—especially if you make the giant version, which makes one feel so dainty ("Oh, I'll just have one"). We like bittersweet chocolate chips, but these are great with any kind of chocolate.

Makes about 2 dozen giant cookies or 4 dozen regular ones : : **Vegan Option**

2 cups white whole wheat flour or unbleached all-purpose flour (or 1 cup of each)

1 teaspoon baking soda

1 teaspoon kosher salt

4 ounces (1 stick) unsalted butter or vegan butter stick (such as Earth Balance), at room temperature

½ cup canola oil or melted coconut oil

¾ cup organic granulated sugar

¾ cup packed organic dark or light brown sugar

2 large eggs or (for vegan) flax eggs (page 141)

2 teaspoons vanilla extract

3 cups old-fashioned rolled oats

1 cup walnut or pecan halves, coarsely broken or chopped

2 cups (1 [10- to 12-ounce] package) bittersweet chocolate chips (vegan, if desired)

Preheat the oven to 375°F. Line a baking sheet with parchment paper. In a medium bowl, combine the flour, baking soda, and salt, whisking to blend.

Combine the butter or vegan butter and oil in a large bowl. Add both of the sugars and, using an electric mixer on medium speed, beat to blend until fluffy. Add the eggs or flax eggs and beat to blend. Add the vanilla and beat to blend. Add the dry ingredients in three additions, beating well after each, until incorporated. Add the oats 1 cup at a time, beating to blend after each addition. Add the walnuts and chocolate chips and mix just until incorporated.

Drop the dough by ¼-cupfuls (for giant cookies) or generously rounded tablespoonfuls (for regular cookies) onto the prepared baking sheet. Use your palm to gently flatten each cookie to a ½-inch thickness. Bake the cookies until just turning golden brown on top, 10 to 12 minutes. Transfer to a rack to cool. Serve warm or at room temperature. The cookies freeze well. Let cool completely, then transfer to an airtight container or freezer bag and freeze for up to 2 weeks. Thaw at room temperature or reheat in the oven just before serving.

Texas Sheet Cake with Mocha Frosting, Toasted Pecans, and Toffee

With apologies to traditionalists, I like this version of Texas Sheet Cake better than the original. The pecans stay crisp as a toasted topping instead of being stirred into the frosting, and a generous handful of chopped Heath bars never hurt anything. Canola oil stands in for shortening, and instant coffee gives the traditional icing more depth (I sometimes use decaf to avoid caffeinating my children). Serve it in pieces no larger than 3 by 3 inches; this is super rich.

Makes one 13 x 9-inch cake; 12 to 16 servings

Cake

2 cups unbleached all-purpose flour

2 cups organic granulated sugar

1 teaspoon ground cinnamon

1 teaspoon baking soda

1 teaspoon kosher salt

1 cup water

4 ounces (1 stick) unsalted butter

⅓ cup canola oil

5 tablespoons unsweetened cocoa powder

½ cup buttermilk

2 large eggs

1 teaspoon vanilla extract

Topping

6 tablespoons whole milk

5 tablespoons unsweetened cocoa powder

1½ teaspoons instant coffee powder (I use a single-serving packet of Starbucks VIA)

4 ounces (1 stick) unsalted butter

3½ to 4 cups confectioners' sugar

1 teaspoon vanilla extract

1 cup pecans, toasted and coarsely chopped

2 (1.4-ounce) chocolate-covered toffee bars (such as Heath), coarsely chopped

RECIPE CONTINUES

To make the cake: Preheat the oven to 350°F. Oil a 13 x 9 x 2-inch baking pan. In a large bowl, whisk together the flour, sugar, cinnamon, baking soda, and salt.

In a medium, heavy saucepan over medium heat, combine 1 cup of water and the butter, oil, and cocoa powder. Whisk until the butter melts; bring the mixture to a boil, then remove it from the heat.

Pour the hot cocoa mixture over the flour mixture in the bowl and whisk to combine. Add the buttermilk and whisk to blend. Add the eggs one at a time, whisking after each. Whisk in the vanilla.

Pour the batter into the prepared pan. Bake the cake until the center is set but soft and a toothpick inserted into the center comes out clean, 25 to 30 minutes (do not overbake).

To make the topping: While the cake is baking, prepare the topping. In a medium, heavy saucepan over medium-high heat, combine the milk, cocoa powder, and coffee powder, whisking well. Bring to a boil, then remove from heat. Immediately add the butter and whisk until it melts. Whisk in the confectioners' sugar and vanilla.

Let the cake cool for 5 minutes, then pour the warm icing over it, spreading to cover evenly. Sprinkle the cake evenly with toasted pecans and chopped toffee. Let the cake cool completely. Serve it at room temperature or chilled. Can be prepared up to 1 day ahead. Cover and refrigerate.

WINE: Keep the elegant sweetness going with a glass of Lost Oak Portejas, a medium-bodied port that pairs seamlessly here.

BEER: Southern Star Brewing's Buried Hatchet Stout has coffee and mocha aromas *and* flavors that will take this dessert experience way over the top.

Salted Caramel–Coconut Milk Ice "Cream"

I started out making this in pint-size batches, but the family begged for more. And really, if you're going to the trouble, why not turn out a quart? I use a frozen-canister-style ice-cream maker. It takes about 20 minutes for this to reach the texture of soft-serve ice cream; after that, transfer it to a resealable container and freeze it until it hardens. This is great on its own, or sandwiched between two cookies (see page 189). If you're new to caramelizing sugar, it might be easier to start with white sugar, as it's more obvious when it caramelizes. Begin preparing the ice "cream" base well ahead of time so the mixture has time to thoroughly chill before you freeze it.

Makes about 1 quart :: **V • GF**

1 cup organic granulated sugar

2 (13.5-ounce) cans full-fat organic coconut milk

1 tablespoon vanilla extract

½ teaspoon (scant) kosher salt

Combine the sugar and ½ cup of water in a medium, heavy saucepan over medium-low heat, stirring until the sugar dissolves.

Increase the heat to medium and bring the mixture to a simmer, allowing it to bubble vigorously. As the sugar cooks, swirl the pan occasionally and use a pastry brush dipped in water to brush down the sides of the pan to prevent crystallization. Simmer the sugar mixture until it thickens and darkens to a deeper caramel color, 7 to 9 minutes.

Turn off the heat and pour in ½ can of coconut milk (the mixture will bubble up vigorously and the caramel will harden). Whisk gently until the caramel is mostly dissolved. Add the remaining coconut milk and stir over medium-low heat until all caramel bits are dissolved and the mixture is warmed through (no need to simmer). Whisk in the vanilla and salt. Remove from the heat. Pour the mixture into a medium bowl or a 4-cup glass measuring cup. Let cool until it's not steaming, then cover it with plastic wrap and refrigerate the mixture until it is cold, at least 2 hours and up to overnight.

Using an ice-cream maker, freeze the ice "cream" according to the manufacturer's instructions. Transfer the dessert to a resealable quart-size container, then cover and freeze until it hardens, at least 2 hours. Can be prepared several days ahead; keep frozen.

Cocoa-Cinnamon-Straciatella Coconut Milk Ice "Cream"

It's surprisingly easy to make vegan coconut milk ice "cream"—the kind that's usually sold for at least $5 a pint—from scratch. *Straciatella* is Italy's answer to chocolate chip ice cream: Melted chocolate is drizzled into the ice "cream" just as it finishes churning, and the ribbons of melted chocolate harden on contact, creating thin flakes throughout. Begin preparing the recipe well ahead of time so the base has time to thoroughly chill before you freeze it.

Makes about 1 quart ice "cream" :: **V • GF**

2 (13.5-ounce) cans full-fat organic coconut milk

½ cup light agave nectar

½ cup unsweetened cocoa powder

½ teaspoon ground cinnamon

½ teaspoon (scant) kosher salt

1 tablespoon vanilla extract

½ cup semisweet or bittersweet chocolate chips (vegan, if desired)

Warm the coconut milk in a medium, heavy saucepan over medium-low heat. Add the agave nectar and whisk until dissolved and the mixture is warmed through (no need to simmer). Add the cocoa powder, cinnamon, and salt, whisking vigorously until completely incorporated and the mixture is hot. Remove from the heat. Whisk in the vanilla extract. Pour the mixture into a medium bowl or 4-cup glass measuring cup. Let cool until it's not steaming, then cover it with plastic wrap and refrigerate the mixture until it's cold, at least 2 hours and up to overnight.

Using an ice-cream maker, freeze the mixture according to the manufacturer's instructions. While the ice "cream" is freezing, melt the chocolate chips in a small, heavy saucepan over very low heat, whisking until melted. When the mixture has achieved soft-serve consistency, keep the ice-cream maker running and drizzle melted chocolate into the mixture as it churns. Transfer the mixture to a resealable quart-size container. Cover and freeze it until it hardens, at least 2 hours. Can be prepared several days ahead; keep frozen.

Apple-Pecan-Oatmeal Crisp

What makes this crisp better than others? Less sugar, which allows fresh fruit flavors to shine through, and a topping that incorporates generous amounts of nuts and oats to make it heartier and more filling. It can be vegan and gluten-free, too (see the ingredients list for substitutions). Apple crisp is the perfect ending to a meal when served with a scoop of vanilla or caramel ice cream or coconut milk ice cream, but if you want to eat it at breakfast, that's your business. And yes, apples grow in Texas. Local Galas can be found as early as late summer.

Serves 8 :: **Vegan Option • Gluten-Free Option**

4 medium-size (2 to 2¼ pounds) crisp tart apples, such as Gala, Granny Smith, or a combination

2 tablespoons organic granulated sugar

1 cup old-fashioned rolled oats (gluten-free, if desired)

1 cup pecan halves, broken into pieces

¾ cup (packed) organic dark brown sugar

¼ cup white whole wheat flour or (for gluten-free) almond meal

1 teaspoon ground cinnamon

½ teaspoon sea salt (only if using unsalted butter)

4 tablespoons (½ stick) chilled unsalted butter or vegan butter stick (such as Earth Balance), coarsely chopped

Ice cream or (for vegan) coconut milk ice cream, for serving (optional)

Preheat the oven to 375°F.

Peel and core the apples and slice them thinly; transfer the apple slices to a large bowl. Sprinkle with 2 tablespoons sugar, toss to coat, and let stand while preparing the topping.

In a medium bowl, combine the oats, pecans, brown sugar, flour or almond meal, cinnamon, and salt, if using; toss to mix. Add the butter or vegan butter and work it in with your fingertips just until large clumps form.

Transfer the apples to a 13 x 9 x 2-inch baking dish. Sprinkle the topping mixture evenly over the apples. Bake until the apples are tender and the topping is golden brown, about 45 minutes (cover the crisp with foil if the topping is browning too quickly). Let cool slightly; serve warm with ice cream, if desired.

WINE: The flavors of lighter desserts, such as this crisp, would be drowned out with most ports and other red dessert wines. Haak Vineyards Blanc du Bois White Port is the perfect alternative. It's aromatic with hints of vanilla, caramel, and mocha.

BEER: St. Arnold Brown Ale features the kind of malty body profile that, while substantial, doesn't weigh down the palate. It's mildly carbonated with a wonderfully rounded mouthfeel.

Almond Butter–Oatmeal Cookie Ice-Cream Sandwiches

The cookies come together quickly with only a few ingredients, and they can easily be made gluten-free and vegan, too. Crunchy raw almond butter and coarsely ground oatmeal give them a rustic, wholesome texture, but they're also good made with creamy almond butter.

Makes 10 to 12 ice-cream sandwiches (about 24 cookies) :: **Vegan Option • GF**

Cookies

1 cup old-fashioned rolled oats (gluten-free, if desired)

1 teaspoon baking powder

¼ teaspoon kosher salt

1 cup organic sugar

1 cup unsalted crunchy or creamy almond butter

1 large egg or (for vegan) flax egg (page 141)

1 teaspoon vanilla extract

Assembly

½ cup lightly toasted raw almonds, coarsely chopped (optional)

About 1 quart vanilla or caramel ice cream or (for vegan) coconut milk-based ice cream (such as Salted Caramel-Coconut Milk Ice "Cream," page 185, or purchased)

RECIPE CONTINUES

To make the cookies: Preheat the oven to 350°F. Line a baking sheet with parchment paper.

In a food processor, pulse the oats into a coarse flour (some texture will remain). Add the baking powder and salt and pulse to combine. Set the dry ingredients aside.

Using an electric mixer on medium speed, beat the sugar and almond butter in a large bowl to blend. Add the egg or flax egg and vanilla, beating well. Add the dry ingredients and beat until incorporated (the dough will be moist yet very crumbly).

Scoop the dough into heaping tablespoonfuls, rolling it gently between your hands to form quarter-size balls. Space the dough balls apart on the prepared baking sheet, gently flattening each with the palm of your hand to ⅓-inch thickness (the cookies will not spread while baking), pushing in the edges lightly to compact the dough. Bake until the tops of the cookies are cracked and drying but the cookies are still soft to the touch, 10 to 11 minutes.

Let cool for 2 minutes on the baking sheet, then use a spatula to gently transfer the cookies to a cooling rack (the cookies will be very tender but will firm up as they cool).

To assemble: If using the chopped almonds, place them in a shallow bowl. Sandwich one packed scoop of the ice cream between two cookies, then squeeze the sandwich together gently to compact the ice cream until it presses out to the edges of the cookies. If desired, roll the edges of the ice-cream sandwich in the chopped almonds. Wrap the ice-cream sandwich in plastic wrap and freeze until ready to serve. Repeat with the remaining cookies, ice cream, and almonds.

Can be prepared up to 3 days ahead. Keep frozen.

Nutty Oatmeal Cookies with Dried Fruit

These big, soft cookies are loaded with goodies. While I like making them oversized as you'd find at a café, they may, of course, be made smaller; just adjust the baking time down a few minutes. We love these with a hot mug of ginger tea.

Makes about 21 extra-large cookies :: **Vegan Option**

1 cup unbleached all-purpose flour

½ cup white whole wheat flour

1 teaspoon ground cinnamon

1 teaspoon baking powder

½ teaspoon baking soda

½ teaspoon salt

4 ounces (1 stick) unsalted butter or vegan butter stick (such as Earth Balance)

⅓ cup melted coconut oil

1 cup organic brown sugar

½ cup organic granulated sugar

2 large eggs or (for vegan) flax eggs (page 141)

2 teaspoons vanilla extract

3 cups old-fashioned rolled oats

¾ cup sweetened shredded coconut

¾ cup chopped raw pecans

½ cup chopped dried apricots

½ cup sweetened dried cranberries, halved if large

Preheat the oven to 350°F. Line a baking sheet with parchment paper.

In a medium bowl, whisk both flours, cinnamon, baking powder, baking soda, and salt to blend.

Using an electric mixer, fitted with a paddle attachment, beat the butter or vegan butter and coconut oil on medium speed in a large bowl to blend. Add both sugars and beat to blend. Add the eggs or flax eggs, beating well after each, then beat in the vanilla. Add the dry ingredients in two additions, beating well after each addition. Add the oats and beat well. Add the coconut, pecans, apricots, and cranberries and mix long enough to incorporate.

Using a ¼-cup measure, drop the dough onto the prepared baking sheet, spacing about 3 inches apart. Use your palm to gently flatten each cookie to a ½-inch thickness. Bake until the cookies are dry to the touch and just beginning to turn golden on the bottom, 14 to 15 minutes. Let stand for 1 minute, then transfer the cookies to a rack to cool. Serve warm or at room temperature. Can be prepared ahead. Seal in an airtight container for up to 2 days, or seal and freeze.

PARCHMENT PAPER

Parchment paper doesn't seem like the sort of kitchen tool that would inspire passion. Such devotion makes more sense in regard to sexier things, like a handheld kitchen torch or a sleek French coffee press. But I am obsessed with parchment paper to the point that I find it difficult to walk by it at the store without buying more, unable to risk the threat of running out. That's because parchment paper is the ideal liner for all things sweet and savory. My favorite use is to line the bottom of a big pan of vegetables to roast. It's naturally nonstick, so the browned bits of onions and potatoes that tend to stick to the dish—jeopardizing the most flavorful part—are left intact, meaning both better-tasting veggies and easier cleanup. A circle of parchment paper to line the bottom of a cake pan makes for foolproof removal. I also use it for baking cookies, lining loaf pans for quick breads, wrapping cheese, and just stacking things that might otherwise stick together. Its one limitation: No broiling allowed. As my son reminded me recently, in a bit of wisdom gathered from the late Ray Bradbury's *Fahrenheit 451*, paper burns at just above 450°F.

Classic Carrot Layer Cake with Lemony Cream Cheese Frosting

Sometimes, classic is best. This is a favorite birthday cake at my house—and any cake that's ever chosen over chocolate definitely deserves a spot in the recipe rotation. Lining the cake pans with parchment paper rounds makes removing the cakes foolproof.

Makes a two-layer round cake; about 12 servings

½ pound (about 3 large) organic carrots, peeled

2 cups unbleached all-purpose flour

1¾ cups organic granulated sugar

1 teaspoon baking powder

1 teaspoon baking soda

1 teaspoon ground cinnamon

½ teaspoon ground ginger

½ teaspoon kosher salt

¾ cup light olive or canola oil

4 large eggs or flax eggs (page 141)

Lemony Cream Cheese Frosting (page 194)

Oil the bottom and sides of two 8- to 9-inch round cake pans. Cut out two parchment paper rounds and fit into the bottom of each cake pan.

Using the grating attachment on a food processor or using a large box grater, grate the peeled carrots (you should have 2½ to 3 cups of loosely packed, grated carrots).

Preheat the oven to 350°F.

In a large bowl, whisk the flour, sugar, baking powder, baking soda, cinnamon, ginger, and salt to blend. In a medium bowl, whisk the oil and eggs just to blend. Add the oil mixture to the dry ingredients and whisk to blend well (the batter will be very thick). Add the grated carrots; using a rubber spatula, fold the carrots into the batter until evenly incorporated. Divide the batter between the two prepared cake pans

and bake until a tester inserted into the center of each comes out clean, 30 to 32 minutes. Cut around the edges of the cake pans to loosen the sides and let the layers cool for 15 minutes in the pans. Turn out the cake layers onto a cooling rack, peel off the parchment paper rounds, and let cool completely.

Place one cake layer on a cake plate. Top the cake layer with one third of the frosting, spreading it evenly over the top. Place the second cake layer atop the frosted first layer. Frost the top and sides of the cake with the remaining frosting.

Can be prepared up to 2 days ahead. Cover with a cake dome and chill. Remove from the refrigerator about 1 hour before serving.

Lemony Cream Cheese Frosting

Fresh lemon juice and zest lend a nice citrusy tang that offsets all the richness of a traditional cream cheese frosting. This also works nicely piped atop the All-Natural Red Velvet Bundt Cake (page 198).

Makes 2 generous cups

4 tablespoons (½ stick) unsalted butter, cut into pieces

1 (8-ounce) container cream cheese

¼ teaspoon very finely grated lemon zest

1 tablespoon freshly squeezed lemon juice

1 teaspoon vanilla extract

⅛ teaspoon kosher salt

3 cups organic confectioners' sugar, or more as needed

Using an electric mixer on medium to high speed, beat the butter until softened. Add the cream cheese and lemon zest and beat to blend. Beat in the lemon juice, vanilla, and salt. Beat in the confectioners' sugar, one cup at a time, adding more by ¼ cupfuls if needed to achieve the desired consistency. Can be prepared up to 2 days ahead of time. Cover and refrigerate. Let stand at room temperature to soften before using.

Pecan Sandies

My childhood was influenced by the 1970s health food craze, so we were more likely to have peanut butter balls made with wheat germ and honey than we were to have store-bought cookies. But on occasion my mother would buy Keebler Pecan Sandies. Now I make a homemade version using the basic shortbread dough that's behind Mexican Wedding Cookies. This recipe also works well with vegan butter, but if you go that route, remember to skip the salt. Prepare the dough with confectioners' sugar for a more compact texture or granulated sugar for a larger crumb. If you really love pecans, press a pecan half into the top of each cookie just before baking; it will toast nicely as the cookie bakes.

Makes about 30 cookies :: **Vegan Option**

1 cup raw pecan halves

8 ounces (2 sticks) unsalted butter or vegan butter sticks (such as Earth Balance)

½ cup organic confectioners' sugar or organic granulated sugar

1 tablespoon vanilla extract

¼ teaspoon salt (skip if using vegan butter)

2 cups unbleached all-purpose flour

½ cup organic granulated sugar, for coating

Preheat the oven to 350°F. Line a baking sheet with parchment paper.

Coarsely grind the pecans in a food processor, or finely chop by hand.

Place the butter or vegan butter and confectioners' sugar in a large bowl and, using an electric mixer on medium speed, beat to blend. Add the vanilla and salt, if using, and beat to incorporate. Add the flour and beat to blend. Add the ground pecans and beat just until incorporated.

Place the ½ cup of granulated sugar in a shallow bowl. Roll the dough into 1-inch balls, roll them in the sugar, and place them 2 inches apart on the prepared baking sheet. Using the bottom of a glass, flatten each cookie to about a ½-inch thickness. Bake until dry to the touch and golden brown on the bottom, about 18 minutes. Transfer to a cooling rack to cool.

Rustic Strawberry Tart

As with all desserts that spotlight fresh fruit, the season's best berries make this tart shine. This dessert was inspired by a large basket of spring strawberries from Fall Creek Farm in Granbury, Texas, where Cullen and Ashley Crisp's mantras are "the smaller, the sweeter" and "the redder, the better." If you're purchasing the grocery-store variety, pony up for organic—it's worth it.

Makes one 10-inch tart :: **Vegan Option**

Crust

1 cup unbleached all-purpose flour, plus more for rolling out

⅓ cup white whole wheat flour

3 tablespoons plus 1 teaspoon organic granulated sugar, divided

⅛ teaspoon kosher salt (skip if using vegan butter)

4 ounces (1 stick) unsalted butter or vegan butter stick (such as Earth Balance)

¼ cup plus 2 tablespoons ice water

Filling

1 pound fresh organic strawberries, hulled and halved

3 tablespoons organic granulated sugar

2 tablespoons cornstarch

1 tablespoon freshly squeezed lime juice

To make the crust: Combine the flours, 3 tablespoons of the sugar, and salt, if using, in a large bowl; whisk to blend well. Cut the butter or vegan butter into ½-inch pieces. Add the butter or vegan butter to the flour mixture and work in with your fingertips until a coarse meal forms (do not overwork the dough; some large bits can remain).

Using a fork, stir in just enough of the ice water to form a dough. Knead the dough briefly until it comes together. Pat the dough into a round disk, cover with plastic wrap, and refrigerate it until you're ready to roll it out.

To make the filling: Preheat the oven to 425°F. Place the strawberries in a medium bowl. Sprinkle the strawberries with the sugar, cornstarch, and lime juice; toss to coat.

Place a large sheet of parchment paper on a work surface; sprinkle it with flour. Place the dough disk in the center of the parchment paper and, using a rolling pin, roll it out to a 13-inch round. Lift the parchment paper up and transfer it, with the crust, to a baking sheet. Spoon the strawberries into the center of the dough, drizzling with a bit of the juices from the bottom of the bowl. Fold about 1½ inches of the edges of the tart dough in toward the center, partly covering the strawberries. Sprinkle the top crust around the edges with the remaining 1 teaspoon of sugar. Bake the tart until the crust is golden brown and the filling is bubbling, about 25 minutes. Let stand for at least 15 minutes (the center will be very juicy but it will set some as it cools). Serve warm or at room temperature.

All-Natural Red Velvet Bundt Cake

The highly circulated "Red Velvet" recipe was popularized by Adams, an extracts and food coloring company out of Austin that offered a free recipe card for the campy cake to promote its products many years ago. I've never been able to bring myself to make the version with an entire bottle of food coloring, but have to admit that, having skirted around that issue, this is one striking, fun, and funky dessert. Only the baker will know that this cake's gorgeous deep red hue comes from puréed beets; a little acidity in the batter keeps them a brilliant red even after baking. Use the vegan frosting recipe below or, if you prefer your red velvet with Lemony Cream Cheese Frosting, see page 194.

Makes one large Bundt cake; about 12 servings :: **Vegan Option**

Cake

1 pound (3 large or 4 medium-size) fresh red beets

2 tablespoons freshly squeezed lemon juice

Nonstick baking spray

2½ cups unbleached all-purpose flour, plus more for coating pan

½ cup natural unsweetened cocoa powder

2 teaspoons baking powder

¼ teaspoon kosher salt

2 cups organic granulated sugar

1 cup organic coconut milk (from a 13.5-ounce can; reserve the remainder for the frosting)

½ cup canola oil

1 tablespoon vanilla extract

½ cup dark chocolate chips (vegan, if desired)

Frosting

4 tablespoons (½ stick) cold unsalted butter or vegan butter stick (such as Earth Balance)

¼ cup organic coconut milk (from a 13.5-ounce can)

½ teaspoon vanilla extract

Pinch of kosher salt

1½ cups organic confectioners' sugar

To make the cake: Scrub the beets and place them in a single layer in a medium, heavy saucepan. Add enough water to cover the beets. Cover the pot and bring to a boil. Lower the heat to low and simmer, covered, until a knife slides easily through the beets, 45 to 50 minutes. Pour the beets into a colander to drain. Run cold water over the beets to cool them. When the beets are cool enough to handle, peel the skin off, cut the flesh into large chunks, and place it in the bowl of a food processor. Add the lemon juice and purée the beets, scraping down the sides of the bowl and processing again, until the beets are completely puréed. (You will have about 1¾ cups of beet purée.)

Preheat the oven to 350°F. Spray a 10-cup Bundt pan with nonstick baking spray or oil it generously. Dust the inside of the pan with flour, shaking out any extra.

In a medium bowl, whisk the flour, cocoa powder, baking powder, and salt to combine. In a large bowl, combine the beet purée, sugar, coconut milk, canola oil, and vanilla. Using an electric mixer on medium speed, beat the wet ingredients well.

Add the dry ingredients and beat just until incorporated. Fold in the chocolate chips. Pour the batter into the prepared pan.

Bake the cake until puffed and set in the center, and tester comes out clean, 60 to 65 minutes. Let cool in the pan for 30 minutes, then cut around the edges and turn out the cake onto a cooling rack.

To make the frosting: Slice the butter or vegan butter into pieces and place it in a medium mixing bowl. Using an electric mixer on medium to high speed, beat the butter to soften it. Add the coconut milk, vanilla, and salt and beat until fluffy. Add the sugar, ½ cup at a time, and beat until incorporated. (The frosting can be thinned with additional coconut milk if you'd rather drizzle than pipe it.) Using a rubber spatula, spoon the frosting into a plastic bag. Snip off one corner and use the bag to pipe the frosting decoratively over the cake. Can be prepared up to 2 days ahead. Cover and refrigerate. Serve at room temperature or chilled.

Buttermilk Pie

Relatively speaking, Martindale, Texas, makes San Marcos (the closest city to Anthony) look like Las Vegas. It's a small town, but it has a restaurant—Cottonseed Café & Deli—with food so delicious that it'd give any big-city restaurant a run for its money. Case in point: This old-fashioned and irresistible buttermilk pie. The recipe comes from Cheryl Soderquist, co-owner and chef, who always emphasizes the freshest, most flavorful ingredients on her seasonal menus. The pie is really rich, so serve it in small wedges with a handful of fresh berries on the side, if you like.

Makes 1 pie; 8 to 10 servings

Crust

1⅓ cups unbleached all-purpose flour, plus more for rolling out

½ teaspoon kosher salt

4 tablespoons (½ stick) cold unsalted butter, diced

¼ cup vegetable shortening (look for organic nonhydrogenated)

6 tablespoons ice water

Filling

5 large eggs

2 cups organic granulated sugar

2 tablespoons unbleached all-purpose flour

1 teaspoon vanilla extract

⅔ cup buttermilk

4 ounces (1 stick) salted butter, melted

To make the crust: Place the flour and salt in a food processor and pulse to combine. Add the butter and shortening; pulse until the mixture resembles coarse meal (do not overprocess). Add the ice water in a slow stream, pulsing just until the dough comes together. Turn out the dough onto a well-floured board. Form the dough into a disk, enclose it in plastic wrap, and refrigerate it until cold, at least 30 minutes. The dough may be refrigerated for up to 2 days or sealed in an airtight container and frozen for up to 3 months.

Lay a large square of parchment paper on a work surface and sprinkle it lightly with flour. Place the chilled dough disk in the middle of the paper and sprinkle the dough lightly with flour. Roll the dough out into a 13-inch round. Transfer it to a 9-inch pie plate. Trim any excess overhang and tuck the edges under, crimping them decoratively. Prick the bottom of the crust with a fork, and refrigerate it while you prepare the filling.

To make the filling: Preheat the oven to 350°F. Whisk the eggs in a large bowl to blend. Add the sugar, flour, and vanilla and whisk until combined. Whisk in the buttermilk.

Slowly add the melted butter, whisking constantly. Pour the filling into the unbaked piecrust. Bake the pie until the top is golden brown, puffy, and beginning to crack, and the filling is set around the edges (it will be slightly jiggly in the middle), 45 to 55 minutes. (The melted butter will be visible in the center of the pie, but after the pie cools, it will redistribute.)

Serve the pie slightly warm, at room temperature, or chilled. Can be prepared up to 2 days ahead. Cover and refrigerate.

Toasted Coconut–Brown Rice Marshmallow Bars

Who knew that these childhood favorites could be vegan as well as gluten free? Dandies brand vegan marshmallows (available at Central Market, Whole Foods, and online) have great flavor. Overheating vegan marshmallows can lead to too-chewy results: Be patient and melt the marshmallows very slowly, and you'll be rewarded with treats that are every bit as good as the original version, but without any questionable ingredients.

Makes about 15 :: **V • GF**

1 tablespoon coconut oil, plus more for oiling baking dish

¾ cup sweetened shredded coconut

4 tablespoons (½ stick) vegan butter (such as Earth Balance)

1 teaspoon vanilla extract

1 (10-ounce) bag vegan marshmallows (such as Dandies vanilla-flavor vegan marshmallows)

5 cups brown rice cereal (not puffed rice; look for Barbara's Organic Brown Rice Crisps, Rice Krispies Gluten-Free Whole Grain Brown Rice Cereal, or Nature's Path Crispy Rice; you will need most of a 10-ounce box; check label for gluten-free, if desired)

Using a little coconut oil, oil a 13 x 9 x 2-inch glass baking dish. Lightly toast the shredded coconut.

Melt the butter in a medium, heavy pot over medium-low heat. Add the coconut oil and stir until melted. Lower the heat to low, and stir in the vanilla. Stir in the marshmallows, allowing them to spread out in single layer, and cover the pot, stirring every 3 to 5 minutes, until the marshmallows soften and melt (the texture will remain a little lumpy), about 15 minutes total. Turn off the heat.

Add 3 cups of the rice cereal and toasted coconut to the marshmallows; using a rubber spatula, fold the cereal and coconut into the marshmallow mixture. Add another 2 cups of cereal and fold in until all the cereal is incorporated.

Transfer the warm mixture to the prepared baking dish and use your fingers to gently press it into an even layer. Let cool slightly. Cut into fifteen squares and serve warm or at room temperature. Can be prepared up to a day ahead. Seal in an airtight container at room temperature.

FROZEN WATERMELON

Sometimes in Texas it gets hot. Like, triple digits for weeks on end hotter-than-hell hot. It's times like those that call for frozen watermelon. Slice a seedless watermelon in half through the stem end, then into quarters. Slice between the watermelon and the rind, and then slice 1-inch-thick triangles from the watermelon quarters. Push a Popsicle stick or wooden chopstick firmly into each watermelon triangle. Line a baking dish or sheet with parchment paper, and place the watermelon pops on the paper. Freeze until solid, then let stand at room temperature for a few minutes before serving.

DRINKS

I'm considered the "drinks" guy because I have spent most of my years in Texas writing about wines, beers, and spirits produced right here in the Lone Star State. I'm not a professional mixologist, so what follows is a mixed menu of original drinks that I entertain with at home, some reimagined classic cocktails, and a couple of seriously terrific contributions from both friends and talented bar professionals around the state. —Anthony

Cowtown Shandy

I'm not suggesting any Texas beer needs to be enhanced, but there's also no need to just let well enough alone. "Shandy" is the British name for a popular German thirst-quencher of equal parts light-flavored beer (such as lager or pilsner) and carbonated lemon-lime soda. Over the past few decades, a seemingly endless number of variants have emerged using lemonade, ginger ale, orange-flavored sodas, and even mineral water. The choice of beer is also up to individuals, although wheat beers are most often used. When I'm bartending, I choose Blood & Honey American Wheat Ale from Revolver Brewing in Granbury, just south of Fort Worth, which is made with local honey and Texas blood oranges. When combined with (nonalcoholic) ginger beer and a generous squeeze of juice from a blood orange, this shandy becomes a summertime quaff with tremendous personality.

Makes 2 servings

12 ounces beer

12 ounces ginger beer

1 blood orange, halved

Slowly pour equal parts beer and ginger beer into each stein. Squeeze the juice of ½ blood orange into each stein and serve.

White Port and Club Soda

This simple, refreshing libation was inspired by the Blanc du Bois Port from Haak Vineyards, near Galveston. The off-dry port made from the white Blanc du Bois grape features notes of peaches and almonds. Delicious on its own, this white port becomes something entirely different according to whatever you choose to accentuate it with. A generous squeeze of juice from just about any fruit will do; try fresh peach, orange, lemon, strawberry, or my favorite, tangerine.

Makes 1 serving

2 ounces white port

2 ounces club soda

2 tangerine slices

Pour the port and club soda into a rocks glass filled with ice. Squeeze in the juice from the tangerine slices and stir.

Hot Dr Pepper with Dark Rum and Cherry Brandy

If Texans ever vote for an official state soft drink, it'll be Dr Pepper in a landslide. It was invented in Waco by pharmacist Charles Alderton in 1885. The recipe remains secret but you can find out nearly everything else about the soft drink at the three-story Dr Pepper Museum in Waco. That's where I first tasted Hot Dr Pepper, a popular cold-weather drink in Texas in the 1960s and '70s; some folks even swore by its curative properties against winter colds. Others added a little white rum to the mix for a drink called a "Boomer." For modern-day Peppers, I add a few more flavors to the soft drink's original twenty-three, including Treaty Oak Aged Rum's seductive vanilla and cinnamon notes.

Makes 1 serving

4 to 6 ounces Dr Pepper

Lemon wheel

1 ounce dark rum

1 ounce cherry brandy

2 dashes of Bar Keep Baked Apple Organic Aromatic Bitters (optional)

Heat the Dr Pepper to 180°F in a medium, heavy saucepan over high heat. Remove from the heat. Place the lemon wheel in the bottom of a heatproof glass or coffee mug. Add the hot Dr Pepper, rum, brandy, and bitters, if using.

Rye Russian

White Russians are simple to make at home and tasty. Deep in my soul, though, I'm a whiskey man, which is why I replace the vodka with rye. Rye whiskey, such as Yellow Rose Straight Rye Whiskey from Houston, features soft, sweet, and mild spice notes that enliven the coffee flavor. This cocktail is kind of like a drink called a "Sneaky Pete," except those are typically made with twice as much cream (or milk) as anything else in the glass. I keep the same proportions as a White Russian and choose traditional Kahlúa Coffee Liqueur.

Makes 1 serving

1½ ounces rye whiskey

¾ ounce coffee liqueur

¾ ounce light cream or half-and-half

Pour all the ingredients into a rocks glass filled with ice. Stir thoroughly.

Robert Lee Shot

My brother-in-law Thomas absolutely loved his West Texas ranch, located just outside Robert Lee. And whenever our families camped at Robert Lee, we camped in a place I referred to as "life without training wheels." There was no running water, no utilities, and no help for miles and miles if something ever went wrong. This drink is my tribute to Thomas, who passed away at age forty-one, and to the place that made him stand his tallest. You can substitute silver tequila for the mescal, and simple syrup for the prickly pear syrup.

Makes 1 serving

¾ ounce mescal

½ ounce freshly squeezed lime juice

½ ounce Prickly Pear Simple Syrup (page 213)

Dash of hot sauce

Place all the ingredients in a low-ball glass and serve.

Prickly Pear Simple Syrup

The prickly pear cactus grows all over Texas, including in my front yard. In the fall, I turn the little torpedo-shaped fruits into simple syrup, which makes a heck of a nice margarita and gives other drinks a beet red color and a fresh, sultry melon flavor. Unfortunately, removing the prickly needles from the fruit's skin is labor intensive and, to be quite honest, frustrating; the best tool for harvesting and handling the fruit before cooking is long-handled tongs. You can either burn off the needles with a small butane torch (which is quick and doesn't hurt the fruit's flesh) or scrub them off with a stainless-steel scouring pad.

Makes about 1½ cups syrup

1 cup peeled and coarsely chopped fresh prickly pears (about 6 ounces)

1½ cups water

1 cup organic granulated sugar

Slice each prickly pear fruit lengthwise through the skin; peel off entire skin and discard. Chop the remaining fruit into small segments. Bring all ingredients to a boil; lower the heat and let simmer until sugar dissolves, about 15 minutes. Let cool to room temperature. Strain the syrup through a double layer of cheesecloth or a fine-mesh strainer into a mason jar. Prickly pear syrup will last refrigerated up to 1 month.

SIMPLE SYRUPS

The basic bar staple known as simple syrup is made from sugar and water and used to soften the rough edges of some bitter spirits. An increasing number of simple syrups available in the "mixer" aisles of liquor stores and grocery stores are using fresh fruits, honey, herbs, and spices for flavoring. When making simple syrups at home, a good rule of thumb is to add the same amount of new ingredients as sugar. But depending on the flavoring, it may be necessary to increase the water by up to ½ cup to ensure the syrup's consistency.

Basic Simple Syrup

Makes 1½ cups syrup

8 ounces (1 cup) water

8 ounces (1 cup) organic granulated sugar

Bring the water and sugar to boil in a heavy small saucepan. Lower the heat to medium-low and simmer until the sugar is dissolved, stirring occasionally, about 10 minutes. After cooling, simple syrup can be stored in a mason jar in the refrigerator for up to 1 month.

Sangria Rosa

Texan David Alan is an accomplished mixologist who helped revamp one of my favorite bars in San Antonio, the Esquire Tavern. In 2013, he published his highly regarded *The Tipsy Texan: Spirits and Cocktails from the Lone Star State*, which includes this sangria. I love it for three reasons: (1) David's letting me reprint the recipe here; (2) he uses St-Germain, an elderberry-flower liqueur from France that has grapefruit, pear, and tropical fruit aromatics and flavors; and (3) when David's the bartender he uses a hollowed-out watermelon for the serving bowl. To make a large block of ice, pour an inch or so of water into an appropriately sized plastic container and place in the freezer; add another inch of water every three hours until almost filled. The slow pace prevents the expanding ice from cracking the plastic. Keep container in the freezer for at least 24 hours prior to serving. Release the ice by warming the container's exterior with a hairdryer.

Serves 8 to 10

2 bottles rosé wine

16 ounces (2 cups) St-Germain elderflower liqueur

1 quart seasonal fruit and berries, such as watermelon, Ruby Red grapefruit, and peaches, cubed

1 watermelon, hollowed out, for serving (optional)

Large block of ice

8 ounces (1 cup) carbonated water

Combine the wine, St-Germain, and the cut fruit in a 1-gallon container. Place in the refrigerator and allow the fruit to macerate for several hours, if time allows.

Transfer to a punch bowl or a hollowed-out watermelon and add the block of ice. Add the carbonated water just before serving. Serve with a ladle, making sure each portion is garnished with some of the cut fruit.

My Paloma

The Paloma is among Mexico's most brilliant libation creations: Refreshing in its simplicity, yet exciting for its beautiful marriage of flavors. You can replace the grapefruit juice and club soda here with grapefruit soda, as is often the case in Mexico, but I think freshly squeezed Ruby Red grapefruit juice adds richer flavor and turns the drink the color of a Texas sunset.

Makes 1 serving

3 ounces Ruby Red grapefruit juice

2 ounces silver tequila

½ ounce freshly squeezed lime juice

Pinch of salt

3 ounces club soda

Lime wedge for garnish

Combine the grapefruit juice, tequila, lime juice, and salt in a collins glass with ice cubes. Top with club soda. Stir gently but thoroughly. Garnish with a lime wedge.

Classic Margarita

Although many of us call it the National Cocktail of Texas, the margarita has become America's favorite cocktail. There are so many variations and flavors to keep track of, including substituting Prickly Pear Simple Syrup (page 213) for Cointreau, but there is only one classic way to prepare it.

Makes 1 serving

1½ ounces tequila

½ ounce Cointreau

1 ounce freshly squeezed lime juice

Lime wedge for garnish

Pour the tequila, Cointreau, and lime juice into a cocktail shaker with ice. Shake well and pour, including the ice, into a glass. Garnish with a lime wedge.

Maurice-a-rita

Because the margarita is so ubiquitous in bars and restaurants and homes throughout Texas, the classic recipe is constantly being reimagined to highlight nearly any flavor. This heat-'em-up version was created by our friend Maurice Hamel and gets a spicy kick from jalapeños.

Makes 1 serving

3 slices jalapeño pepper with seeds, plus more for garnish

3 (¼-inch-thick) slices hothouse cucumber, plus more for garnish

2 tablespoons freshly squeezed lime juice, divided

Pinch of salt

2 ounces silver tequila

½ ounce Cointreau

2 teaspoons agave nectar

Splash of freshly squeezed orange juice

In a cocktail shaker, muddle the three jalapeño slices and three cucumber slices, 1 tablespoon of the lime juice, and the salt. Add ice, the remaining 1 tablespoon of lime juice, and the tequila, Cointreau, agave nectar, and orange juice. Shake well for 15 seconds and strain into a chilled, salted margarita glass. Garnish with thin slices of cucumber and jalapeño.

Ruby Port, OJ, and Tonic

I discovered a version of this recipe in a very old book from the 1940s. People used to add a lot of sugar to their cocktails, no matter what was being created. For today's tastes, a little tonic water and bitters make this very appealing for warm weather. The Texas Ruby Port from Woodrose Winery is my favorite choice for this drink.

Makes 1 serving

2 ounces ruby port

2 ounces orange juice

Dash of Angostura bitters

Tonic water

Into a large glass filled with ice, pour in the port, orange juice, and bitters. Strain into a rocks glass without ice. Add the tonic water to fill. Stir gently.

My Michelada

A traditional Mexican Michelada is crisp beer poured over ice with a healthy squeeze of lime—simple and refreshing. But once the drink migrated north of the border to Texas, bartenders started adding savory and spicy elements until the Michelada was transformed into more of a southwestern-style drink. My Michelada gets its kick from Cholula hot sauce and assorted spices. Although the beer loses clarity, it gains savory character that matches well with many Tex-Mex dishes.

Makes 1 serving

3 tablespoons freshly squeezed lime juice

2 teaspoons vegan Worcestershire sauce

1 teaspoon hot sauce

1 teaspoon low-sodium soy sauce

½ teaspoon freshly ground black pepper

½ teaspoon chili powder

10 to 12 ounces beer (ideally, light-flavored)

Lime wedge for garnish

Combine the lime juice, Worcestershire, hot sauce, soy sauce, pepper, and chili powder in a cocktail shaker with ice. Shake well and strain into a lightly chilled pint glass.

Add the beer, slowly. Garnish with a lime wedge.

Cortez the Killer

Jason Stevens (of Bottled in Bond Consulting) is an Austin bartending legend. I think of him more as a "bar chef," putting a great amount of time, energy, and thought into his cocktail creations. This frosty tiki-style drink is something like a Mexican piña colada. You can find Coco López, tamarind paste, and high-fat coconut milk in specialty foods stores, as well as some grocery stores.

Makes 1 serving

6 to 8 cubes ice

1½ ounces silver tequila

½ ounce mescal

2 ounces pineapple juice

¾ ounce tamarind paste

1¼ ounces high-fat coconut milk

½ ounce Coco López cream of coconut

¼ ounce freshly squeezed lime juice

2 dashes of Bittermens Elemakule Bitters or Angostura bitters

3 coffee beans, crushed, for garnish

Pinch of ground cinnamon for garnish

Pineapple leaf for garnish (optional)

Combine all the ingredients, except the garnishes, in a blender filled with ice and blend.

Alternatively, combine all the ingredients, except the garnishes, in a cocktail shaker filled with ice, shake, and strain into a tiki mug or a tall glass filled with finely crushed ice.

Garnish with the coffee beans, grated cinnamon, and a pineapple leaf, if you have one handy.

SHRUBS

A shrub, sometimes called a "drinking vinegar," is a sweet and tangy syrup made from fruit, sugar, and vinegar. I first learned of shrubs from Caterina Miltenberger, corporate mixologist for Dallas-based Glazer's Wholesale Distributors, who is also something of a cocktail historian. Back in the eighteenth and nineteenth centuries, when our great-grandmothers were canning fruits and vegetables for the winter, they would add sugar and vinegar to the leftovers and make syrups for refreshing warm-weather drinks.

Vinegars add tartness and acidity according to their own flavor profiles: Red wine vinegars and cider vinegars impart broad, dark flavors; whereas white vinegars, such as Champagne vinegar and rice vinegar, remain more neutral but add brightness; and balsamic vinegar provides tangy-savory flavor.

Shrubs can be flavored with citrus fruits, stone fruits, apples, berries, and even prickly pear cactus fruit. But also try ginger, rhubarb, arugula, rosemary, and sweet potatoes, for example, to add an unexpected depth-charge of flavor and tangy complexity to a variety of cocktails and soft drinks.

Basic Shrub

1 cup organic granulated sugar

1 cup vinegar of your choice

1 cup chopped fruit or other ingredient of your choice

Combine and heat the sugar and the vinegar in a saucepan until the sugar dissolves. Add the chopped fruit (or other ingredient) and let simmer for about 20 minutes, stirring occasionally. Let cool and then strain out the solids through a double layer of cheesecloth. Store in an airtight glass jar in the refrigerator or in a cool, dry location for at least 24 hours before using.

Cowtown Shrub

From Caterina Miltenberger, corporate mixologist for Glazer's Distributors in Dallas, comes this modern-day version of a nineteenth-century-style fruit and vinegar drink called a shrub (see sidebar, page 223). It matches intense sweet-tart cranberry flavors with sweet-mellow toasted notes from TX Blended Whiskey from Fort Worth.

Makes 1 serving

2 ounces TX Blended Whiskey

1 ounce Cranberry Shrub (page 225)

4 ounces Topo Chico mineral water or club soda

Fresh blueberries and blackberries for garnish

Pour the whiskey, cranberry shrub, and carbonated water into a collins glass filled with ice.

Stir gently. Garnish with blueberries and blackberries.

Cranberry Shrub

You can add 1 ounce of this Cranberry Shrub to a glass of club soda and ice for a sweet-tangy soft drink. It's delicious in other drinks, too, like the Cowtown Shrub (page 224).

Makes about 1 cup shrub

1 cup fresh or frozen cranberries

1 cup organic granulated sugar

1 cup white cider vinegar

Muddle or bruise the cranberries. Place in a large saucepan. Add the sugar and vinegar and heat over low heat, stirring occasionally, until the sugar is dissolved, about 15 minutes. Turn off the heat and cover the saucepan. Let sit for 24 hours in the refrigerator or at room temperature.

Pour into a blender and liquefy. Strain the shrub through cheesecloth into a mason jar. Can be prepared ahead. Cover and refrigerate for up to 1 month.

Holiday Glühwein

Laura's husband, Till, was born in Germany, and the fall after they married they headed to Hamburg to visit his aunts. As they wandered through the falling snow in the outdoor Christmas markets, Till bought them mugs of Glühwein (pronounced GLUE-vine), or "glow wine." The hot, spiced red wine lives up to its name, especially as German vendors offer it *mit Schuss*—with a shot of rum. Not only does Texas have a rich history of German culture (early immigrants in Hill Country had their own dialect), the state also gets very icy come winter, which makes Till's take on this warm wine so welcoming.

Serves 6

2 cups water

¾ cup plus 2 tablespoons organic granulated sugar

3 sticks cinnamon, coarsely broken

10 whole cloves

½ whole nutmeg

½ large orange (preferably organic, as you'll be using the peel)

2 (750-mL) bottles inexpensive dry red wine (such as Cabernet Sauvignon)

Rum (optional)

Place the water and sugar in a small, heavy saucepan. Enclose the cinnamon sticks, cloves, and nutmeg in a large mesh tea ball, breaking the cinnamon sticks to fit as necessary.

Place the orange half on a work surface. Using a knife, cut large strips of peel away from the fruit, avoiding most of the pith (reserve the peeled orange half for later).

Add the filled mesh tea ball and the orange peel to the sugar mixture. Bring to a boil, stirring occasionally to dissolve the sugar, then lower the heat to low and simmer for 10 minutes. Remove from the heat.

Pour the spiced syrup mixture, along with the mesh tea ball and orange peel, into a medium, heavy pot. Add the wine. Squeeze the juice from the peeled orange half into the wine (taking care to avoid adding any seeds). Heat the mixture over medium heat, stirring occasionally, until hot (do not boil). Remove the mesh tea ball and orange peel, discarding the spices and peel. Ladle the Glühwein into mugs, adding a shot of rum to individual servings as desired. Serve hot.

Formulas for Metric Conversion

Ounces to grams . . . . multiply ounces by 28.35
Pounds to grams . . . . multiply pounds by 453.5
Cups to liters . . . . multiply cups by .24
Fahrenheit to Centigrade . . . . . subtract 32 from Fahrenheit, multiply by five and divide by 9

Metric Equivalents for Volume

U.S.	Metric	
⅛ tsp.	0.6 ml	
½ tsp.	2.5 ml	
¾ tsp.	4.0 ml	
1 tsp.	5.0 ml	
1½ tsp.	7.0 ml	
2 tsp.	10.0 ml	
3 tsp.	15.0 ml	
4 tsp.	20.0 ml	
1 Tbsp.	–	15.0 ml
1½ Tbsp.	–	22.0 ml
2 Tbsp. (⅛ cup)	1 fl. oz.	30.0 ml
2½ Tbsp.	–	37.0 ml
3 Tbsp.	–	44.0 ml
⅓ cup	–	57.0 ml
4 Tbsp. (¼ cup)	2 fl. oz.	59.0 ml
5 Tbsp.	–	74.0 ml
6 Tbsp.	–	89.0 ml
8 Tbsp. (½ cup)	4 fl. oz.	120.0 ml
¾ cup	6 fl. oz.	178.0 ml
1 cup.	8 fl. oz.	237.0 ml (.24 liters)
1½ cups	–	354.0 ml
1¾ cups	–	414.0 ml
2 cups (1 pint)	16 fl. oz.	473.0 ml
4 cups (1 quart)	32 fl. oz.	(.95 liters)
5 cups.	–	(1.183 liters)
16 cups (1 gallon)	128 fl. oz	(3.8 liters)

Oven Temperatures

Degrees Fahrenheit	Degrees Centigrade	British Gas Marks
200°	93°	–
250°	120°	–
275°	140°	1
300°	150°	2
325°	165°	3
350°	175°	4
375°	190°	5
400°	200°	6
450°	230°	8

Metric Equivalents for Weight

U.S.	Metric
1 oz	28 g
2 oz	58 g
3 oz	85 g
4 oz (¼ lb.)	113 g
5 oz	142 g
6 oz	170 g
7 oz	199 g
8 oz (½ lb.)	227 g
10 oz	284 g
12 oz (¾ lb.)	340 g
14 oz	397 g
16 oz (1 lb.)	454 g

Metric Equivalents for Butter

U.S.	Metric
2 tsp.	10.0 g
1 Tbsp.	15.0 g
1½ Tbsp.	22.5 g
2 Tbsp. (1 oz)	55.0 g
3 Tbsp.	70.0 g
¼ lb. (1 stick)	110.0 g
½ lb. (2 sticks)	220.0 g

Metric Equivalents for Length

U.S.	Metric
¼ inch	.65 cm
½ inch	1.25 cm
1 inch	2.50 cm
2 inches	5.00 cm
3 inches	6.00 cm
4 inches	8.00 cm
5 inches	11.00 cm
6 inches	15.00 cm
7 inches	18.00 cm
8 inches	20.00 cm
9 inches	23.00 cm
12 inches	30.50 cm
15 inches	38.00 cm

INDEX

Note: Page references in *italics* indicate photographs.

MEATLESS IN COWTOWN

MEATLESS IN COWTOWN